Dedicated To

All the single ladies, enjoy your journey, keep your heart open, never settle, and never lose your sense of humor!

My Parents, who allowed me to grow up in a house where true love existed, and specifically my Mom who supported my journey, no matter how hard it may have been to witness as a parent

John S, without your desire for round table story-telling sessions at MMS and your consistent begging for a book, I would have never even thought to put pen to paper.

Jill, for your never ending creative brilliance (yes, you can take full credit for the title), for reading every last word despite what you have on your own plate, and for giving me true writer's notes – the good, the bad, and the ugly – my story would not have come together without your guidance.

John I, for taking interest, believing, and dedicating months of your time to helping me bring this to life.

Marissa, for living through it all, side by side, for not always understanding but never going anywhere, and for standing up proudly in the end #samelife

All Of My Friends and Relatives mentioned, thank you for being a part of my journey… and for allowing me to write about you.

And to **one more person**, whose dedication comes with the conclusion, and not a moment before or it will spoil the whole story

Prologue

"That Girl"

From the year's 2002 through 2012, I was THAT girl. You know the one. The girl that would show up to any family holiday, wedding, or party solo and would be met with questions like "Why are you still single?" or "Why hasn't anybody snatched you up yet?" or "You are pretty, successful, smart, out-going, and a nice person... why are YOU here alone?" These questions both baffled and annoyed me. I wanted to reply with "If I knew the answer to that, I'd likely not be here alone", but I always ended up turning a shade of red, gave them a shrug, and walked away feeling badly about myself. The questions typically came with a tone of accusation, like there had to be some underlying reason why I was single and I was the one who had the key to unlock the mystery for these people so that they could sleep better at night knowing the "truth". I will never understand asking single people such questions and I vow to never become the person who does that kind of asking.

While I am no model, I'd say I would be described by most as either cute or pretty, depending on whom you asked. Standing at 5'4, slim, long brown hair, and big brown eyes, my best feature has always been my butt; which to this day always amazes my Mom and her side of the family who have what we have creatively labeled as "basses" (backs that go straight in to their ass). But not me; I inherited the round butt from my Dad's side of the family and it has been the focal point of what has attracted most of the men I have been with to me. To boot, I was lucky to have a lot of amazing friends and my career had progressed with ease; I was promoted every two years or so and somehow escaped the lay-offs of 2000 and 2005. I was able to travel and experience so many wonderful and amazing things in life and always felt truly blessed for all of it. My life was full in every aspect except one area -- the love department.

The truth was, I wasn't looking to just find a husband. Anyone can find a husband. I was looking for the real deal... that deep connection, chemistry, respect, adoration, and unconditional kind of love. I needed to love and be loved unconditionally in order for me to be able to make a commitment to someone "forever". I knew that anything less would not work and I could not walk down the aisle without all of it. So while I knew what I actually wanted and needed, I don't think I, or my family and friends, truly understood that this kind of love was something that COULD possibly take a lot longer to find.

They say you have to kiss many frogs before you find your prince. But when "many" became "too many" was still left to be determined...

Introduction

"Mr. Almost But Not Quite Right"

When I first graduated college and moved to New York City, I did not want a boyfriend. My friends and I were having such a great time going out, enjoying our new independent lives in a big city with so many possibilities, that the last thing I wanted was a relationship. Sure I was casually dating and having fun meeting different guys but at 22, a serious relationship was the furthest thing from my mind.

But as the saying goes, "When you're not looking for it, that's when it happens..."

About four months into my first job, my boss Suzanne decided she was going to set me up with one of her good friends. He was five years older than I was and therefore I assumed more mature (this was before I learned assuming makes an ASS out of you AND ME!). He was from a nice family in Connecticut and, as Suzanne described him, "cute, funny, and smart".

I was flattered she wanted to set me up because it meant she liked me, but because I wasn't interested in meeting a guy who was out to find a serious relationship, I felt reluctant. However, how could I tell my boss I wasn't interested? Could I really tell the person that offered me gainful employment "Thanks, but no thanks." I had a myriad of thoughts going through my head about what would happen if I refused. "Could I get fired?" "Would she no longer like me, and maybe even make my life miserable at work?" While I would eventually become very close to Suzanne and know the answer to those questions would have been no, at the time, I did not. So I determined I had no choice but to go along with this, no matter what.

On November 17th, 1999, with half of my company looking on (how embarrassing!), we were introduced at a benefit on the West Side. And while I tried to fight it, there was no denying the immediate chemistry between us. He was 6'2, which was very appealing to me. I loved tall guys. I know many taller women despised women like me who were 5'4 and only dated guys who were 5'10 or taller, but it was what I was attracted to. He had dark hair, big hazel eyes, and a presence that drew me right to him. While the first question he asked me, "So Courtney, what is your favorite movie?" was typical and likely straight from a Dating 101 book, by the end of the evening, he had me laughing A LOT.

By Christmas we were an official couple — meeting friends, families — the whole nine yards. Within the first 3 months he flew me down to Florida to meet his grandma and many extended cousins. And just like that, I found myself in the "dreaded" relationship. When my Mom reminisces about this particular time, she always says, "He rushed you. He was calling me mother-in-law and you were not even engaged!" While she was right, I got swept right up in to it. He was showing me off like I was the best thing since sliced bread and being a Leo, I ate up every bit of it.

We were blissfully happy, hardly ever fought, laughed a lot, and all of my friends and family members adored him, as he was quite the charmer. I was completely swept off my feet and assumed the feelings I was having would just continue for the rest of my life. I could not fathom anything bringing us down from Cloud 9, and I fed right in to everyone else's belief that we were "Done" and down the aisle within the year!"

But after about nine months, the extended honeymoon we were on came to an end and the reality of life hit. He was miserable at work and with the market taking a hard turn south, on the verge of losing his job. My once charming, animated, affectionate light-hearted boyfriend turned sad, disheartened, and aloof. Being 23, I had no idea how to deal with any of it. At the time, I believed I was being supportive, but in hindsight, I had not yet developed the knowledge or tools to be. After all, my dating experiences up until that point had been isolated to high school and college, where "dating" meant going to my boyfriend's house in sweats to watch football on the couch with ten of his closest buddies lying next to me on a regular basis. This was my first "real world" relationship and I was far from prepared for what was to transpire over the next few months.

As my boyfriend became more and more down, he pulled further and further away from me. And the more I wanted things to just "go back to the way they were", the farther away from that they went. The relationship was on a downward spiral, but I was so invested by that point I was unable to come to terms with the fact that it was no longer working. I sat in it until he broke and ended things… for the first time.

We started to play what I would later realize were the games many men and women play when they do love someone, but not enough to really make it work "forever". We would break up, cease all communication, he would miss me, make a huge grand gesture, such as call my mom at 3am looking for me on New Year's Eve and upon finding out I was in Vermont skiing, go to a car rental place thinking he would drive there to "find me." Yes folks, that happened. It was always somewhere on that fine line between hopelessly romantic and over the top dramatic. And I would fall for it every time, believing things were actually fixed and could go back to the way they were. This "routine" went on for about six months until I finally grew tired of it. His long emails in between break ups, the promises he would make, they all eventually started to fall on deaf ears. I had finally succumbed to the fact the relationship was never going to work, and no matter how much effort I put in to avoid the failure I felt, it was over.

It was at that point in time when I felt my world had come crashing down. I had thrown myself into the belief that I was supposed to have been swept off my feet by this person I had thought was my prince charming; when reality sunk in, it was not pretty. At twenty-four and a half I was not equipped to deal with a real world break up. So I did what I believe many twenty-something broken hearted girls do… I frequented Barnes & Noble looking for every self-help book ever written which I was naive enough to actually believe held all of the answers to life's problems. Sitting on that bookstore floor was about the only time I felt safe and comforted during those next few months. Yes, you can think it — hell, I'll even say it — I was Pathetic with a capital "P."

Was I not the one that didn't even initially want the serious relationship? How on Earth I had gotten myself all wrapped up in to this mess, I had no idea. And I was pretty certain my ex did not spend time reading self-help books or torturing himself on what he could have done differently. All men had to do was throw themselves into their work and they could shut out anything else that may be going on in their lives. It amazed me how they were able to shift their focus to one thing only, while women could do 10 things simultaneously all while wallowing over their failed relationship.

But like with most things, time healed my wounds. And by my 25th birthday, I was ready to move on to bigger and better things. For the first time in a long time, I was excited and believed I was truly ready to let go of *Mr. Almost But Not Quite Right*, put all the drama that came with him behind me, and meet someone new. Unfortunately, I had no idea what was in store for me — in my wildest dreams, I could never have imagined the true realities of single life.

I actually get the biggest kick out of the girls who met their husband on the dance floor at Lot 61 when they were 24 and hammered and say they were "once single and understand." They think because they partied for a couple of years, had their assorted random hook-ups and flings, and went out four or five nights a week that they understood the trials and tribulations of dating. Speaking from experience, and on behalf of my fellow thirty-something single friends, I can stand here proudly on my soapbox today and tell you with absolute certainty those are the women that have no clue whatsoever. I can say all of this because I lived the single life in New York City for eight years and another two in Chicago. At 35, I had more dating experiences than I ever thought possible. And anyone who has said it's easy has absolutely no idea what he or she was talking about.

But in truth, without the experiences I had I wouldn't have had the meetings, dates, relationships, and conversations with friends and family that not only helped shape me, but also gave me all of the material I can now share with you. As you embark on my dating journey, I hope you find both humor and helpful hints in my story. Whether you're a woman recovering from a three-year relationship gone south or a guy trying to figure out why date number one never lead to date number two, I hope my experiences help shed light, understanding, and the feeling that you are not alone in the "shark eat shark" world of dating. And maybe, just maybe, it will help squash all of those family members, friends, friends of friends, and co-workers from asking those same questions year after year about WHY perfectly normal girls are single for so long!

Frog #1

"Mr. Nervous"

Dating for the first time after you get out of a serious relationship is definitely a little strange, especially when all of the dating experiences you have had have been either with serious boyfriends or people you dated in the bubble I call college. So, when I got back on the dating scene for the first time post break-up with *Mr. Almost But Not Quite Right*, I was nervous. Still, I went in thinking I would probably end up in another serious relationship pretty quickly — that it would be just as easy as the last time.

First dating lesson learned: Never assume anything based on the past.

A friend of mine offered to set me up with a friend of her boyfriend. I had met my ex-boyfriend on a set-up, so I figured what the hell, why not? Phone numbers were exchanged and he called a day later. I remember thinking "Just like that I have a date — this is going to be easy!"

He did not live in the city so it was up to me to pick a place to go, and as luck would have it, there was a cute Italian restaurant right across the street from my apartment. I thought it would be a great romantic spot for a first date.

He called my cell around 7:30 that Friday night, and five minutes later I was headed to meet the guy I hoped would be the next love of my life. I was having a great hair day, I had a cute new outfit on for the big occasion and I was feeling confident getting back on the dating scene. Things were working. I was ready. I was excited.

Unfortunately, within seconds of meeting this guy, I realized I was doomed.

I did not find him the least bit attractive. But worse than that, the guy was so nervous that he was profusely sweating to the point I was not even sure I wanted to shake his hand hello, let alone hug him. All I could think was, "What was my friend thinking?" It all actually made me wonder if I was the first date he had ever been on. I don't think I had seen a guy that nervous since my first kiss in the sixth grade.

As much as I knew I was going to hate every second of the next ninety minutes of my life, I had to be polite and have dinner with this guy. After all, he did drive all the way into the city from Connecticut. So, we sat down to dinner and I made my virtuous attempt to at least have a good time. But it turned in to a monumental struggle. Just having a normal conversation had become nearly impossible because every time I looked at *Mr. Nervous*, all I saw was sweat — perspiration pouring down his face, his neck, through his shirt. He started to move around a lot in his seat too, which started to make me nervous. Nothing about this date was comfortable.

On top of my own agony, the waiter clearly noticed the situation too because he continued to drop off napkins every time he passed our table. I was mortified to be having dinner with this guy in public. And while that might sound a bit shallow, I was the girl on a dinner date with a guy who looked better suited for an appearance in a deodorant commercial than in the Italian restaurant across the street from my apartment. Oh God, help me!

Needless to say, I lost any appetite I may have had by the time napkin number three was put in play. By that point, my focus was simply surviving the meal and figuring out how I was going to get my friend back for setting me up on this escapade. Unfortunately, this also made me look like the typical anorexic New York snob who made guys take her out to a nice restaurant only to barely touch her food. My no-win situation was getting gloomier by the minute.

Finally, after what seemed like the longest meal of my life, the bill came and I started to see the light at the end of the tunnel. Ten more minutes and I would be home watching a movie on my couch — by myself.

As I started to daydream about curling up with my blanket and a tub of ice cream, I was unceremoniously interrupted by, "Courtney! Hello, Earth to Courtney!" Had he been talking to me this whole time? Apparently, the bill had actually come and was already paid for. Oops.

But since I had completely tuned him out, my mind quickly got excited — there was no way he would want to spend another second with me either. Just as my hopes were rising, they were met with the ten worst words I could have heard: "So, do you want to go somewhere else for a drink?"

The moment of truth for this evening was here, and now I had to think. Would it be politically correct for me to say to a guy I met a mere two hours earlier that if he really thought I was going to be seen in public with him for one more second, then he would have to go home and shower first? His once nice baby blue shirt had large spots of navy as a result of his clear and present sweating issue. The thought of me giving him a hug goodnight made me shudder.

I had an internal debate with myself about whether I should address this with him as he awaited my response, but I quickly decided it was better to leave sleeping dogs lie. "I am actually really tired. Long day. You know how it is." Smile, smile. Bottom line, I really was not ready to sign onto dating someone who had the potential to prevent me from eating and enjoying future meals at good restaurants without a Sham Wow — I frankly loved eating way too much to take that much of a risk.

Ten minutes later, after an awkward good-bye (I will spare you the gross details; let's just say hand sanitizer), I found myself curled up on my couch with that bowl of Häagen-Dazs ice cream, watching a movie. Alone. If only I knew then that this was to become my Friday night ritual for years to come…

Second dating lesson learned: Never go out for dinner on a blind date. It is much faster to chug a vodka tonic in five minutes versus having to eat an entire chicken breast with mashed potatoes.

However, the date had provoked my thoughts on the art of the set-up. People did not necessarily think about who you were and who you may like when they decided to set you up with someone. I suddenly found myself part of this "singles" club I had heard many of my single friends talk about. People in relationships really thought if you were single and they knew a single guy, then it was absolutely obvious that the two of you should go out. It was a deluded theory, but one I quickly realized had become my new reality.

Frog #2

"Mr. Cheap"

About a month after that first date, I was out with some friends at a bar on the East Side. I was having a great time when this guy approached me as I was ordering my second vodka tonic of the evening. After talking for a while, he asked for my number. He seemed nice enough, so I figured what the hell, I could hand over my digits. I had to get back in to the dating scene and I could not let one bad date keep me from meeting Mr. Right. Besides, I was only on my second drink — there was no way my beer goggles had come out just yet. My judgment could still be trusted…couldn't it?

He called two days later and we made plans for the following Wednesday evening. At the time I worked on the Upper West Side, so he agreed to meet me at my office so we could grab a drink around there. On my dating scale of 1-10, the date was at a six for most of the evening; not half bad for a first date. After nearly drowning at the table in the Italian restaurant a month prior, I quickly learned not to expect fireworks right off the bat. Good conversation that flowed with minimal long silences meant serious potential for a second date, which I found happening as we both enjoyed our cocktails. But that second date was never going to happen with this guy; when the bill came, my six quickly became a one.

Third dating lesson learned: Do not determine the status of a date until it is 100 percent completely over.

I must say I am really not all that old-fashioned. I can open a door for myself, I can order for myself, I did not need a man to stand up every time I got up from the table…the list could go on. However, and I must stress this was a <u>big</u> however, when it came to first dates, I still believed in some chivalry — namely that the guy would pick up the tab. I always offered, but I did so with the premise that he would not accept. There were some dating traditions that I (and many others) still found sacrosanct. Unfortunately *Mr. Cheap* didn't quite adhere to that same belief system. He might as well have asked me to pay for the entire date and his cab ride home. When the bill came, he looked at it and said, "Ok, you got 25 bucks?" I swore for a split second I had heard him wrong.

After taking a moment to gather myself from his stunning request, I looked in my wallet and realized all I had was a $20 bill. I let him know thinking he would realize it seemed a bit much to take from me, especially since I had one beer while he slugged back three gin and tonics. But to my surprise, it did not even faze him, and *Mr. Cheap* calmly extended his hand for my money.

This was absolutely appalling to me. He obviously was not even taking a second to think that if he took my last $20 I may not have cab fare home. I was infuriated and confused all at the same time.

I held back saying any of this to him. Instead, I handed over the $20 note, got up from the table and walked right out without even saying good-bye. I firmly believed that actions spoke louder than words and, when it came to dealing with men, that statement was especially true. Walking out would definitely make a larger statement and the miser would get the message…or so I thought.

This guy was as relationship savvy as a baseball player is about biochemistry. He ran after me and appeared completely confused, stumbling his way to ask me out again. When I turned down the second date, he was even more confounded. "I don't understand! We seemed to have such a great time." What I wanted to scream at him was more along the lines of "Actually, you, your gin, and my cash had a terrific night together."

It was pretty obvious that he needed to find himself a Dating 101 book and spend some serious time studying, especially if he was ever going to have a prayer of getting a second date in NYC!

Frog #3

"Mr. Shallow"

After a few more failed set-ups for one reason or another, some friends insisted that I look to online dating to improve my luck. Several of them pressed me to go on J-Date, and while it took a lot of persuasion, I finally decided to take the plunge (Note: I am Jewish). I accepted the fact that I was going to have to broaden my horizons when it came to dating in NYC, primarily because of my realization that dating was not quite as simple as I had envisioned just a few months earlier.

On a rainy Saturday afternoon my best friend Marissa helped me put my profile together. We searched through every photo album to find the perfect pictures to post and, after just a few hours, I felt I was ready to conquer the world of online dating. To my surprise, I started to receive quite a few e-mails from a number of guys immediately. But, being a J-Date virgin meant I was unaware of the need to have a screening process and was pretty quick to give my phone number to just about anyone who contacted me.

Fourth dating lesson learned: Online dating is a completely different animal — hold back in giving out your phone number so readily.

This one guy in particular seemed to stand out and I got pretty excited about him. He was actually taller than 5'7", a few years older and a successful lawyer. He was quick-witted over email and he seemed to be normal enough. He was also very open about the fact that he was as skeptical of online dating as I was, and I think in some way that made me feel a little better as well. So, when he asked, I gave him my number.

Two nights later, I was at home getting ready to watch some Thursday night TV when my cell phone rang. It was the J-Date guy— how exciting! He was in his car driving home from Brooklyn and told me he was about to pass my apartment.

He wasted no time and got right in to it:

"Since I am about to pass your apartment, do you think you can run downstairs so I can take a quick look at you before we set up a date?"

Fifth dating lesson learned: Never tell an online date exactly where you live before you have even met them

I didn't quite drop the phone, but had to take a minute to make sure I heard him correctly. Was this guy for real? I mean skepticism was one thing, but how shallow could you be? Was I supposed to go downstairs and stand in front of him like a model while he critiqued every inch of my body and decided if I was good enough for him to take on a date? While I was just as skeptical of the online dating scene as the next person, there was no way I was going to ask someone to give me a drive-by preview before I decided I was going to go out with them.

It had taken me all of ten seconds to decide there was no way I was going out with *Mr. Shallow* in this lifetime. I politely said that I was in bed and it was not a good time for me — I then proceeded to screen his calls for the next three weeks until he finally got the picture and left me alone. The end.

Interlude

"Miss Disappointed"

As we entered the new millennium, instant gratification was something we had all become so used to in every aspect of our lives. The Internet and email let us connect to anyone around the world, groceries could now be delivered to our door with the click of a mouse on our increasingly portable laptop computers, and cell phones meant you could be available at any time. But my new dating experiences got me thinking: in a world where everything seemingly could be attained so easily for us, why had finding a new boyfriend become so impossible? I realized online dating was not necessarily going to be the quick fix to my dating woes — especially when I had possible online dates doing drive-by's to judge my date worthiness. I had mistakenly believed that the possibility of meeting people on line was immediately going to increase my chances of finding "the one". Dating was something I had once imagined to be really exciting: meeting all sorts of different guys from various walks of life, having the pick of many suitors, getting wined and dined and spoiled; instead it was proving to be anything but. Maybe I had watched too many episodes of Sex And The City. It was becoming quite clear that reality dating was quite different than the 30-minute make believe I was glued to every Sunday night on HBO.

Frog #4

"Mr. Critic"

While my feelings of defeat were still hovering, I had never been known to be someone who gave up easily. So while my first few online experiences were not great (*Mr. Shallow* of course being the worst), I psyched myself up again, dismissed *Miss Disappointed*, and re-engaged in the world of J-Date. After all, I did know people who had met their spouses on the web.

Within a day or so I had met another guy and once again I was hopeful! We wrote back and forth a few times over email before I threw it out there, "Do you want to meet up?" I learned that it was not worth investing too much time before meeting; if there was going to be a real connection, we had to make it in person and not in cyber-space.

He agreed, but asked to go on a lunch versus evening date. This was a first for me and it meant I was not going to be able to have a drink to relax. Even if we were having a good time, we were going to have to watch the clock because I had to make it back to work. Given these facts, the odds were not really stacked up well in this guy's favor, but I figured it was worth giving him the benefit of the doubt, and it was something different for me too. So with only some minor trepidation, I agreed to meet him for a lunch date.

Sixth dating lesson learned: An alcoholic drink is an absolute necessity when going on a first date, especially a J-Date.

We met at a sushi restaurant on the Upper West Side near my office. I got there first, and after twenty minutes of waiting, he finally arrived. Anyone who knew me knows being late, especially any more than five minutes, was one of my biggest pet peeves. It was off to a rocky start AND he was down to fifty minutes— never good to have the clock ticking on a date.

When he finally arrived, I was taken aback by who stood before me. He was wearing a long trench coat, his jet black hair was slicked back with more hair spray than I thought a single bottle contained, he wreaked of Drakkar, he had a cell phone in one hand and blackberry in the other, and wore black sunglasses so I couldn't see his eyes. Looking like Tony Soprano's right hand man, I began to wonder if I had made a mistake and set up a date with a guy from La Costra Nostra's singles site! Still, I told myself to relax and just go with it. I was only going to have to spend at most, forty minutes with this guy. Plus I would be able to enjoy some good sushi, which had become one of my favorite cuisines.

We followed the waitress to our table and before I even had a chance to sit down, he blurted out, "You know, you look much better in person than you do in your profile. You should go home right now, take a picture of yourself and post that instead." If that was a compliment intended to make it easier as we got things started, he certainly didn't phrase it well. Or perhaps I should have been insulted that he was insinuating I did not look good in pictures?

I would not have the chance to respond and find out — apparently he had a lot more advice to share. He went on to explain to me why I looked better in person. He critiqued my angles. He told me how I should pose. What was supposed to be an introductory sushi lunch date had turned into a full-blown modeling critique of my online pictures and profile. I was so stunned by the conversation I was speechless and actually let it go on for thirty minutes before I came to the conclusion that I was not on a date with a Mob Boss... it was the J-Date Nazi!

I had lost any interest I had a chance of ever having in this guy. And to be quite frank, he was in no position to be giving me advice on my looks. Brad Pitt he most certainly was not. I was completely over him and this lunch date. Lucky for me, he had enough decency to pay. At the very least, I got a good, free sushi meal out of this deal.

Seventh dating lesson learned: Always be wary of someone who wants to meet for lunch on a blind date.

Since finding a relationship-savvy first-date was going nowhere I began to wonder how many more lessons I would have to endure in this game of dating. Thankfully at that time I did not know the answer; if I had, I may have reconsidered dating all together!

Frog #5

"Mr. Head Bop"

You can't catch a fish if you don't have a line in the water, right? Whether it was a setup, online or a random meeting in a bar, I had made a promise to myself to continue to approach new opportunities with optimism despite the fact my first few months on the dating scene had proved very unsuccessful. My father used to always say that no matter what happened, I should never become closed off to the possibility of finding someone — never become cynical. With that in mind, when Marissa offered to set me up with "a great guy", I agreed.

I met up with this "great guy" for a drink one night after work at the Bryant Park Hotel. I was impressed with his choice. The atmosphere and music were great for a first date. There was only problem with this evening.... Him.

Within minutes of introducing ourselves, it became pretty obvious that this guy was on something, and I don't mean the chair he was sitting on. His eyes were completely glazed over, he was not focused and his speech was somewhat slurred. And while he delivered on what I considered the hot factor, with his long, lean body, wavy brown hair, tanned face, and deep blue eyes, it was clear this "great guy" was more than just high on life. It was amazing how quickly a cute guy could turn ugly just by his actions and demeanor.

My excitement for the evening had quickly gone from a 10 to a 2. Instead of sitting across from me at the table, he sat down right next to me, making it completely impossible to have a conversation. He wanted to "watch the DJ and everyone getting down" — always a positive sign on a first date. Carrying on a conversation with him was impossible, because he was completely incapable of stringing together more than two or three words. In fact, the only thing he seemed to be able to do at all was dance in his seat. As the music got louder, he proceeded to do what I referred to later as a "head bop" dance, a cross between a child on a pogo stick and a central park pigeon, for most of the evening. My only regret about this date was that I didn't have a cell phone capable of recording video so that I could put it on YouTube and see how viral it could become. It was pretty obvious that he was more into the music than me.

Still, I attempted to get his attention and start a conversation. After all, I was under the impression we were supposed to be on a date. Together. But it was apparent that his idea of a date meant he showed up completely high on something and that we were supposed to connect through "feeling the music." I think the most I got out of him conversation-wise the entire night was "Great beat they got going on here, huh?"

This was certainly not my idea of fun, and after an hour of watching this guy do the "head bop", I finally decided I could not take it anymore. I elected to play the "I'm really tired" game because I just could not take one more second of this. So I let out a big yawn and said, "I can't seem to keep my eyes open. I was up for a good portion of the night and it all just hit me now. I'm so sorry but I'm going to have to head out."

I don't know if he even really heard me over the loud music. And I'm certain he did not notice that I had left. But at that point, I really did not care. As soon as I hailed a cab, I called Marissa to ask what on earth she was thinking. Her response — "I am completely shocked he acted like that" — led me to question her character judgment and made me doubt if I would let her set me up again anytime soon. Unless my goal was to go out with every shmo out there, I was going to have to be more selective in whom I was allowing my friends to set me up with.

Eighth dating lesson learned: Get a detailed description; "He's a GREAT guy" will no longer cut it!

After this last situation, I began to question the setup even more. At the end of the   day, it was no different than a sales pitch. Those initiating the set up would use words like "handsome" or "great" or "successful" to describe the product they were selling you. And just like in business, when given a positive presentation, you were typically sold.

But the reality was, OF COURSE they were going to tell you only positive things. Would you buy something someone described in a negative light? No, you wouldn't. And it became glaringly obvious to me that this whole salesmanship was now being applied to dating.

Simultaneously I had come to the realization that the people who were setting me up were already IN relationships and often complained that they did not have other fun couples to go out with. I had suddenly found myself questioning if my friends were just looking to pawn me off on the first semi-decent guy they knew just so they would have another couple to dine with.

The only problem with that scenario… I would have rather eaten alone…

Frog #6

"Mr. Arrogant"

After *Mr. Head Bop*, and all of the epiphanies that had come with him, I decided I needed a little break from dating. Nothing drastic — I was not suddenly taking a vow of celibacy — but I needed to rejuvenate myself and regain my desire to meet the opposite sex. So, when this new guy started working at my media agency, the last thing I wanted was for him to ask me on a date.

Ninth dating lesson learned: It is possible to find what you DO NOT want even when you are NOT looking.

The new guy seemed nice enough to have as a friend and I was always willing to be open and friendly to anyone who started to work with our team. I was not one to exclude people from our lunch chats or not invite someone in the office out for an after-work drink. The way I saw it, I was just as friendly to him as I was to everyone else.

Unfortunately this guy had another agenda.

It all started one day when I was complaining at the office that I needed my air conditioner installed in my bedroom because I was dying of heat every night. My best guy friend was supposed to help me out with this annual task, but he had been stuck late at work all week — and my sheets and I had paid the price during the hot, muggy New York City summer we were having.

"I'll come over and do it for you tonight," was all my new co-worker said, and just like that, he was in my apartment a few hours later. I felt a little bad having a guy I had just met come over to help me, but at the same time, I really did need my air conditioner installed. Sleeping with a wet towel on my head to keep cool was certainly not working. Besides, I thought he was just doing me a favor and being nice, trying to make a friend at work.

However, as soon as he finished, his true motives came out. Matter-of-factly, he asked, "So why don't you and I date?" Just like that, he was in my face about dating. I suddenly found myself completely trapped. The walls in my VERY small room felt like they were closing in on me and I had no idea what to say. He was not even asking me out on a single first date, but instead insinuated we should be DATING?! As in dates plural. Multiple dates.

Aside from having zero interest in dating him, I also did not want to get involved with someone at work. The last thing I needed was to get caught up in an office romance. I liked to keep my personal life, well — personal. So, after taking a quick second to put my thoughts together and compose myself, I took a deep breath and simply said "I really don't think it's a good idea. I think you are a nice guy and I thank you for putting in my air conditioner, but I think we should just leave well enough alone". I assumed this would be enough for him to take his cue and be on his way.

Tenth dating lesson Learned: Never underestimate the persistence of an arrogant man who does not get what he wants.

My answer was not sufficient for him so instead we spent the next two hours arguing in my apartment as to why we should or should not date. He absolutely would not take no for an answer. He was relentless, but not in a romantic kind of a way. He was arrogant, condescending and, quite frankly annoying.

"I really don't understand why you won't go out with me? This is ridiculous! Your reasoning is not valid and I'm not going to accept it!" he repeated numerous times, starting off in a normal speaking tone and eventually screaming the words at me.

I wanted to tell him to go screw himself and kick him out, however I knew I would have to see him the next day, and every day we worked together thereafter. I was attempting to be as politically correct and polite as possible, but with every raise of his voice, the harder it became. The last straw came when he blurted out, "This just makes no sense! I'm a good-looking Jew. What more do you want?"

"A lot more than that, *Mr. Arrogant*!" I screamed back.

I decided it was time to lie and say I needed to run an errand just to get him out of my apartment. Enough was enough with this entire conversation. But even as I headed out on my make-believe run to the store, and was forced to ride with him in the elevator, this guy would not let up. As each floor number lit up, I was met with a remark.

5th Floor - "I am not going to stop pursuing you"
4th Floor - "You should feel happy someone wants to date you."
3rd Floor – "What is wrong with you?"

Six floors down never felt so long in my life. He was relentless and acted as though no other girl had EVER turned him down. It was like I was supposed to feel honored that he wanted to date me.

Anyone who has ever been romantically involved with a coworker (or in my case, had a coworker wish they could be involved with someone) knows this problem was not going to just go away. We had to see each other every day at work. For the next few weeks, he proceeded to speak to our co-workers about it — over and over and over. He had become obsessed, and whether it was because I kept throwing up stop signs and he wanted to run through them, or just because his persona wouldn't allow him to accept "not interested," it was moving from bad to worse.

He actually approached Suzanne, still my boss at the time, and said, "You know, I've dated many girls that are way better looking than Courtney. I just don't understand why SHE won't go out with me!" If *Mr. Arrogant* had any clue, he would have realized he just spelled out the answer for himself. I had reached my breaking point, leaving me no choice but to succinctly tell him he needed to get over it, me, and, more importantly, himself.

After that, we stopped speaking and, as you can imagine, it was a totally uncomfortable work environment. To make matters worse, he had just been assigned to my account! Yes the arrogant stalker had to report to me, as in I was now his boss! It was like I was living a real life Jerry Seinfeld episode.

While it took a tad longer than a 30 minute TV show to end, he eventually could not handle my being his boss and quit after about a month. Thank God he was finally gone from my life forever. However, the realization that I had managed to get myself in to a situation where I had to deal with the remnants of a break up without ever having reaped the benefits of dating left me feeling nothing short of frustrated.

Interlude

"Miss Frustrated"

What ever happened to that sweet innocent puppy love I had experienced in high school? The kind where the guy would do anything in the world for you? He did that not because he felt you owed him something or that you should have felt honored that he was interested in you. He was sweet and bought you a rose to show you how much he liked you. He chased you a bit (and perhaps deep down you made him chase you some), but not in a stalker way. He simply liked you and he wanted to win you over.

I had broken up with my high school boyfriend when I went to college, but it was during this time that I missed him the most. His sweet, innocent persistence was what had gotten me. Should I no longer expect that from guys in their mid-twenties? Were all the men in Manhattan so jaded and full of themselves that they forgot how to be humble? I found myself scared and longing to be 16 again. I was trying to remain optimistic about my options, but my patience had begun to wane.

I was frustrated by the notion of a great relationship —
and my inability to find one. I was frustrated with the
men I was coming in contact with. I was frustrated that
they were rude, arrogant, or just plain weird. How was it
that people around me were in serious relationships with
normal, "good guys" and I kept finding myself with the
exact opposite? Was I doing something wrong? This voice
of self-doubt about my "relationship worthiness" had
started to creep in, and while I didn't want to listen to it, I
noticed it seemed to be getting louder and louder...

Frog #7

"Mr. Perfect On Paper"

Just when I started to feel like my faith in dating and the opposite sex was lost forever, *Mr. Perfect On Paper* walked into my life. And it was *Mr. Perfect On Paper* that I thought could be Mr. Right.

I actually met him at my birthday party and I knew right away I was going to like him. "There is just something about this guy," I kept repeating over and over to my friends. We made eye contact a few times before we spoke and I felt his eyes pierce right through me. Whenever I got that kind of a feeling, I always knew right away there would be an instant connection. When he finally walked over to make his move, the conversation was so easy that it felt like we had known each other for years, and it was validating. He gave me a kind of warm, fuzzy feeling inside that I had not experienced since meeting *Mr. Almost But Not Quite Right.*

Our first date was a low-key sushi restaurant where he introduced me to eel and Saki for the first time. With his glasses and preppy work attire, he was a little more "dorky" than I typically went for, but he was tall (roughly 6 feet) and with his sandy brown, wavy hair, green eyes, and big smile, I found myself wildly attracted to him. To boot, I took a lot of comfort in that we had a lot of people in common; we went to the same college and while we didn't know each other there, we shared connections and he grew up with my cousins in Poughkeepsie. It all felt very safe and easy, a feeling I had not had since being back in the dating pool.

Eleventh dating lesson learned: Perfect on paper does not mean perfect for you.

For the first time I believed I was on the right road to finding the next love of my life. However, I had not in fact pieced together that my motives were not completely on the straight and narrow. In truth, I wanted to be 100 percent over my ex. But because I had taken some steps backwards in the process after my recent string of frustrating dates (which admittedly led me to missing *Mr. Almost But Not Quite Right*), I was sitting more at 95 percent. So when *Mr. Perfect On Paper* came along, I dove in head first instead of taking things slow and really getting to know him. I let myself get completely wrapped up in BELIEVING we had exactly what it took to end up in a serious relationship and assumed he be the solution for finally putting my last relationship completely behind me.

Twelfth dating lesson learned: The demise to all is making something special before it becomes that way on its own.

After we had been dating for a month, he asked me to go to a comedy show followed by a sushi dinner near the theater. Right after the waiter placed my tuna and salmon/avocado rolls on the table, *Mr. Perfect On Paper* turned to face me, took my hands in his, looked deep in to my eyes, and told me he felt we were better off as friends.

I was stunned. He had left me speechless and I could hardly catch my breath. I could not understand what on Earth had happened because in my mind, we were "perfect" for each other. We had the same type of mindset, background, families, experiences…I mean, how could this guy who I completely thought I wanted to be my next boyfriend be breaking up with me?

Me: "I don't understand. What did I do?"

Him: "Nothing. It's not you. It's me."

Me: "But I don't understand. You just introduced me to your parents last weekend."

Him: "That has nothing to do with it. I just don't think I can do this. I'm bad in relationships. I'm very picky and I have made mistakes in the past of dragging things out longer than I should have and I don't want to do that to you."

The rest of the conversation was a bit of a blur because I was having trouble comprehending how something that seemed to be heading in one direction all of a sudden took such a sharp U-Turn. I was distraught. I had been turning guys down left and right, and this guy was actually going to walk away from me?! I mentioned earlier I am a Leo; we do not take rejection well. I went home that night and cried to my roommate and then proceeded to stay up for half of the night delicately crafting an email to send to him. Well if I'm being honest, it was more like a novel. I poured my heart out and told him that if "he just needed time to work through his issues, it was ok. I could give him that time", that "I would be there to work through things together with him", and that "I didn't want him to make a rash decision based on his past experiences."

It got me nowhere. He had made up his mind and none of the thousands upon thousands of words I had sent were going to change the decision he had made. If I had been able to see the truth that had been staring right at me, I would not have been even remotely surprised by what was happening. First, I would have realized that I had built this idea in my head of who I thought *Mr. Perfect On Paper* was (similar enough to my ex minus his issues). Second, I would have realized that should not have been the basis for what I built my next relationship on. And third, I would have realized I did not actually know whether or not he fit the bill because I didn't take the time to find out. I was doomed from the start. While he had been living in reality and figured out quickly we were much better suited as friends, I threw myself into all if it without my usual safeguards, leading to an out of the blue break up for me but a rational decision for him.

As I struggled to make sense of it all in the days that followed, I received a phone call from my ex, *Mr. Almost But Not Quite Right*. He wanted to let me know he was moving, had cleaned out his apartment, and if I wanted the stuff he found of mine, I could come pick it all up the next afternoon from his doorman. While I believed it all a bit odd as I had already gathered all of my belongings the year prior when we broke up, I was curious to see what on earth he had left for me. The next day I dragged my friend Colby the three blocks and one avenue to his apartment to claim my things. When I arrived, I was happy I had brought a strong guy with me as I was met with four huge boxes filled with every little thing I may have ever put my hands on, including old and might I add, used, dishtowels and oven mitts.

After I got over the initial shock of what lay in front of me, Colby and I dragged the junk that was now mine back to my apartment. I stood in my living room staring at the pile of items I had reclaimed and decided I needed to understand what would have possessed him to box this type of stuff up and have me come to take it away. So, I called him and was met with the worst seven words I could have possibly heard after being dumped.

"I'm moving in with my new girlfriend," he blurted out. And then went on to explain he needed to get rid of anything that ever reminded him of me!

Talk about pouring a gallon of salt in to a very open wound! Was this some kind of a sick joke? He was seriously moving in with someone? How could HE have found someone before ME? That was not the way this was all supposed to have worked out! And that was when it all hit me like a ton of bricks: I had subconsciously been in a race with my ex to make sure I wound up in a new relationship first. Because after all, had I been the one to "win", it would have further justified my worth as a girlfriend and his stupidity for having lost me.

Boy, was I in a pickle! I had somehow managed to wake up and figure out I was not as over the aftermath of the break up with my ex as I thought I had been. AND I had to get over the idea that *Mr. Perfect On Paper* was not, in fact, my Mr. Right. All I wanted to do was shoot the vodka straight into my veins to numb the pain. This was a dose of reality I had not been prepared for and it left me feeling very uncertain about my future in dating.

But lucky for me, those good old clichés, "timing is everything" and "things happen for a reason" eventually began to ring their bells loud and clear. And while I wished I had been more in touch with myself sooner, I learned to accept my reality and finally stopped beating myself up over it. *Mr. Perfect On Paper* had been 100 percent spot on, as once I really got to know him better, we truly were much better off as friends; and eventually I would also become close friends with his wife, her twin, and everyone else in their family. Yes, we all lived happily ever after... as friends.

The reality was, after giving it that time I needed to in order to discover my truth, I was able to crawl my way back out of that emotional hole I thought I never would, and started to approach things from a much more honest place. And I was pleasantly surprised to discover none of this meant I had to throw in the relationship towel; there were still some fish left out there for me to catch in the treacherous waters of dating.

Frog #8

"Mr. Best Friend No. 1"

Can men and women really just be friends? This was an age-old question that came up on a regular basis — in books, on TV, in conversations. The truth is, I don't think there is a black-and-white answer to that question because nothing about men and women being friends is black and white. I think if you are really close to someone of the opposite sex, and if the situation allows for it, feelings can develop one way or the other. Anyone who says differently is likely in denial.

So based on my theory, when one of my guy friends professed he had feelings for me, this should not have been a shock. We had known each other since we were kids, went to high school together and stayed in touch through the years. But I actually was sort of surprised. Or maybe just surprised he had the guts to actually come out and tell me. Of course this big announcement came after many, many drinks at his crazy Halloween party where we could hide behind costumes and gallons of alcohol — so maybe he was not THAT gutsy. Regardless, we spent the next half hour in his bedroom making out.

Of course this threw a small wrench in my big plans. I had just gone on my first date with *Mr. Perfect on Paper,* who we now know I thought I was going to marry and live happily ever with in the suburbs with our dog and 2.2 kids. So this grandiose confession did not exactly come at a convenient time. After reading the previous chapter, I'm sure you are thinking going with *Mr. Best Friend No. 1* may have been the better move.

Thirteenth dating lesson learned: Hindsight is 20/20.

But other than *Mr. Perfect On Paper* being in the picture, there were other issues afoot. Unfortunately, or fortunately (however you choose to look at it), we were not the only two still in touch from high school. And there was a part of me that knew that if I went for *Mr. Best Friend No. 1*, I would end up in bed with him and all of our friends. We were still in the phase of life where our friends' thoughts meant a lot, where there was a lot of judging and not a whole lot of supporting going on, and everyone felt they needed to know everything about everyone else. Information was not necessarily a privilege, but rather an expectation. These were not the most conducive of situations in which to formulate a stable relationship.

My point was proven twenty minutes after we started making out. I had to pee, which meant I was actually going to have to leave his room. I actually contemplated not going and holding it. And when I realized that wasn't going to work based on the amount of alcohol I had drank, I even thought about sneaking out of his window. All of these options, as well as about ten others I had come up with, seemed to be better choices than opening the door and seeing all of our friends' faces staring back at us in disbelief.

Eventually I realized I had no choice; unless I was going to end up soaking in my own pee, I had to give in and open the door. And like an episode of Friends, it played out as I foresaw it in my mind. We were met with mouths opened so far they may have been touching the nasty spilled beer filled kitchen floor. The awkwardness of the moment could not have been better scripted in Hollywood.

My girlfriend grabbed me by the arm immediately and dragged me into the bathroom to find out all of the "details." Thankfully she chose the bathroom or I would have peed my pants, which maybe would not have been so bad given it would have deflected me having to answer questions about what I had been doing in *Mr. Best Friend No. 1's* bedroom.

Oh well, too late. I was stuck in the bathroom with her with my pants down (literally and figuratively), dishing the details of my make-out session. I had barely sat on the pot when she began bombarding me with questions.

"WHAT are you doing?"

"Why are you kissing him?"

"Do you like him?"

"Are you guys going to date?"

The barrage continued, and it seemed as if she was never going to come up for air. I felt like screaming "I DON'T KNOW!" but all I could muster up was "I just want to kiss him and kiss him and kiss him." She looked at me like I had fifty heads, but then again she had about fifty heads due to my alcohol intake that evening. Still, even with the help provided by the evening's liquid courage, I don't think she was expecting me to say that. I honestly don't think I was expecting myself to say that. And at the end of the evening, my guess was that we both expected me to chalk it up to alcohol. But deep down, I knew this was not the case.

I think if this situation had occurred later on in my life the outcome may have turned out different. But I was still in my twenties and very concerned with what my friends thought. I was not quite comfortable in my own skin yet and we were all still somewhat immature. I certainly was no exception.

This became quite evident when he finally got up the nerve to ask me out and we went on our first date. He took me to one of my favorite places by my apartment where I proceeded to do one of the worst things I think I have ever done on a date —I divulged the play-by-play details about my first date with *Mr. Perfect On Paper* throughout half of our meal. Who does that and WHY would I have done that? Well, I believed I went this route because first, I was having trouble getting past how *Mr. Best Friend No. 1* and I were going to make this transition from friends to dating. I knew him when he was shorter with no chest hair. We used to play manhunt and marco polo every summer. How was that "kid" going to be my grown up boyfriend? Second, I did not want to give *Mr. Best Friend No. 1* the wrong idea given the newfound excitement about *Mr. Perfect on Paper* I now clearly had.

Fourteenth dating lesson learned: Never rule something out before you have given it a fair chance.

In truth, I should have been mortified by the way I handled the situation. Maybe I deserved all of the horrid date karma past, present and future because of the way I acted that night? To *Mr. Best Friend No. 1's* credit, he went with it and acted like my friend — because at the end of the day, that was what he was and always had been. After dinner we went to a New York Knicks game at Madison Square Garden, where I proceeded to exhibit even more immature behavior. A friend of ours from high school who worked for the Knicks arranged during halftime to put our names on the scoreboard over center court and congratulate us on our engagement. While hysterical after the fact, during it, not so much. I was so embarrassed I tried to hide under my seat, which was horrible behavior for a couple of reasons. First, I made *Mr. Best Friend No. 1* feel as though I was so embarrassed when he didn't seem to be. I was over the top with my level of embarrassment when, in reality, why? Secondly, WHY was I even hiding? No one knew who we were. No one was staring at us (until I tried hiding under the seats). There were no pictures of us. But there I was acting like a ten-year-old because I was uncomfortable — and in truth, also completely afraid of everything this entire night meant and what it could lead to.

Because he knew me well enough, he realized where this was headed and just let it go. We parted ways after the game was over and I never looked back. During that time I never thought perhaps I was making the wrong decision, or that it might be wise to have given both *Mr. Perfect On Paper* and *Mr. Best Friend No. 1* the same shot. That maybe I should have dated them both at the same time instead of going full speed ahead with *Mr. Perfect On Paper* — only to end up single and right back in the same place a month later.

Fifteenth dating lesson learned: What goes around comes around.

A year or so after the infamous Knicks game date, it was payback time. I'm not saying *Mr. Best Friend No. 1* did things to specifically get back at me, but I think it was safe to say that I eventually ended up paying my dues over time. Each of those stories could be chapters of their own — all that would be needed was a quick name swap from *Mr. Best Friend No. 1* to *Mr. Unreliable.* And then a few years after that phase, *Mr. Best Friend No. 1* even became *Mr. Friend With Benefits.*

But that brings us back to the initial question I posed in the beginning of this chapter: Can men and women really be best friends? I believe the answer is that they can, but not without that gray area that usually includes some level of drama and heartache to go with all of the positives that a wonderful friendship provides.

And to this day, that always stood true for us. While we don't get to see each other all that much given we no longer live in the same city, we are very much still friends and always show up for each other for the major milestones of life.

Frog #9

"Mr. Mama's Boy"

You know it's bad when your Mom decides to set you up —
especially when she had never officially met the guy she's setting
you up with. Instead she claimed she "had seen him in passing in my
building, and he looks cute." Apparently she and her neighbor had
become friendly, so being two Jewish yentas they decided it would
be a great idea to setup their single children.

*Sixteenth dating lesson learned: Be weary of your Mother trying to
introduce you to a new friend's son, especially when she's never
even shook hands with the guy herself.*

At the time, I was still recouping from the aftermath of the *Mr.
Perfect On Paper* chapter, and because she told me that this guy
actually looked like *Mr. Perfect on Paper*, I figured I had nothing to
lose. So with only a little hesitation, I agreed that she had the green
light to give this guy my number.

Two days later he called and we set up a date for that Friday night.
There was a part of me that was excited. I was getting back on the
dating scene and if this guy really did resemble *Mr. Perfect On
Paper*, well then maybe I would actually be attracted to him and did
I dare say it, even like him? Wouldn't that just be so easy and
"perfect"?

Because he lived in Jersey, this guy had a car so he picked me up to
drive downtown to dinner. While I was slumped down in the seat of
his sports car, I was not able to get a full frontal view of him, but it
was very easy to see this guy looked NOTHING like *Mr. Perfect On*

Paper. In fact, the only similarity they had at all was that they both wore glasses. He was about fifty pounds heavier and he had what one could refer to as a "Jew-Fro" (think painter Bob Ross's color mixed with Howard Stern's texture). Now if I could tell this from his side profile in the front seat of his car, how was it that my Mom — who had seen him multiple times in her building, as she proclaimed when she was selling me on the setup — could draw this ridiculous comparison? To this day, I believe the caring mom that she was and still is, she just wanted me to move on as quickly as possible and was willing to go to any and all extremes. Mission accomplished Mom.

Seventeenth dating lesson learned: All mothers over the age of 50 should have their eyes checked.

Even worse than his less than attractive physique was his less than stellar personality. I was bored by the conversation before we even made it to the restaurant. This guy had nothing interesting to say, unless of course someone found it interesting that he still was living at home. This was all he seemed to be able to talk about - the fact his mom cooked for him, did his laundry and made his bed. And that turned out just to be the warm-up; throughout our entire meal, all he discussed were the benefits he found from living under his mother's roof. The list went on and on as he made it pretty clear he had no intention of moving out any time soon.

Meanwhile, I was in the middle of this conversation stupefied. Was this somehow supposed to turn me on? Because who isn't attracted to a man who has his mother waiting on him hand and foot at the age of 27! Obviously this was not what I wanted nor what I was interested in. And all the while, I kept asking myself, "What was my Mother THINKING?!" As he blathered on about his life at home with mom, I started to tune him out and fast-forwarded 10 years, envisioning what my life would be like with *Mr. Mama's Boy*. I could see my life mimicking one of those '50s sitcoms, with the wife hanging on her husband's every word while she cooks, cleans and does laundry on a daily basis. Nope this whole scenario was not for me. I wasn't sure what century this guy was living in, but in my world, you graduated college, moved out of the house and took care of yourself — whether you were a guy or a girl. It would be impossible for me to live up to what he had become accustomed to as far as what his mother provided for him — nor would I even want to try and fill that role. I would be set up to fail right off the bat with my less than stellar cooking abilities.

By the time I snapped back from my daydream, the dessert menu had appeared in front of me. The reality was, I could not bear to sit in the restaurant any longer with this guy. I told him I was full even though it nearly killed me to walk away from dessert -- I wanted that warm chocolate soufflé so badly! We had the check within minutes and before I knew it, I was back in my apartment. Alone.

Still, I kept coming back to asking myself how this guy planned on ever having a relationship? He lived at home with his parents! Were the girls he dated supposed to come back to his apartment for some really quiet sex, each time praying his parents didn't walk in on them like they were back in high school? How could someone find that attractive? But I guess I really could not blame my mom for not having sorted out the logistics of how his living situation may have impacted her daughter's sex life. I decided I would let it slide.

That said, I also made another important executive dating decision: no more setups through my Mother.

Frog #10

"Mr. Five Minutes"

Unfortunately "Five Minutes" was not referring to how long this date lasted in bed. And I say unfortunately because that scenario would have actually been much more appealing and one I would have preferred to have found myself in versus the one that I am about to tell you about. In this chapter, "Five Minutes" was instead used to describe one of the shortest dates recorded in the history of my dating life.

It was a Wednesday night after work and I had to go meet a new J-Date guy all the way on the Upper West Side. To help put this in perspective for those of you who have never lived in New York City, getting to the Upper West Side from the East 30's where I lived at the time was similar to traveling to Guam, by kayak; it truly could be considered by some New Yorker's as a long distance relationship. But I agreed to meet him out on his turf.

Eighteenth dating lesson learned: Always stay within five blocks of your home when going out with a guy you are meeting for the first time.

I called Marissa at 8 p.m. during my cab ride over. After a number of failed attempts using J-Date, I really needed a pep talk to get excited. As I got out of the cab, Marissa's last words at 8:15 were "Good Luck! Call me on your way home so I can hear all about it!"

By 8:30, I was back on the phone with her, halfway home. I probably should have listened to my gut that told me trekking to the Upper West Side during rush hour for someone I had never met was not really an advantageous decision — it certainly would have saved me the $20 cab ride there and back.

I walked into the bar and saw him standing a few feet from me. "Hmmm" I thought, he's pretty damn cute! Maybe I shouldn't have been so skeptical." With much higher hopes for the evening, I made my way through the crowd towards the sandy-brown haired guy with dimples I saw standing in front of me. And just as I was about to stick my hand out to formally introduce myself, I heard "Courtney?" come from behind me. I froze for a second and thought, "Do I know somebody else here?" I turned around from the guy I thought was my date for the evening to see a guy quite a bit shorter calling my name. Still somewhat confused, I got a little closer and quickly realized that behind the acne filled face and glasses, THIS was actually my date. I had been duped.

Nineteenth dating lesson learned: The pictures in someone's online profile may not always be a true reflection of what they really look like.

This guy had taken his glasses off, used cover up and lied about his height in his profile. I had heard through other friends that some guys actually did stuff like this, but I just could not understand why. What was the point? You were eventually going to meet and the person was going to find out. All I wanted to do was make a mad dash out of there, but of course my conscience weighed me down. I just couldn't bring myself to call him out on it, so we grabbed a drink and sat down. And believe it or not, from there, things deteriorated even more!

I would say I am a pretty decent conversationalist, and most people who knew or worked with me would agree that I can talk to anyone about most anything. But talking to this guy was more painful than having four wisdom teeth extracted without the benefit of sedation or Novocain. I tried every route: Where did you grow up? Where did you go to college? Tell me about your job, your family, your first pet…All I got were one-word answers and no questions back. With 600 seconds of painful one-way discussion under my belt, I slugged back my glass of wine and decided it was time to go. I got up, shook his hand good-bye and was off like a bat out of hell. I am sure he tried to say something to me as I walked out of the bar, but at that point, it didn't matter.

When I called Marissa from the cab, she couldn't believe we had just spoken only minute's prior. I disclosed all of the details of what had just occurred with *Mr. Five Minutes*, and after I heard myself repeat the minutes I would never get back in my life, I decided I really needed to be <u>much</u> more selective with whom I met on J-Dork, my official new name for J-Date. Marissa cracked up at the name I had come up with, which I found pretty clever if I did say so myself. I just wished I didn't have to call it that -- the implications of J-Dork were far more frightening than funny.

As per usual, Maris talked me down from the ledge I was clearly heading to jump off and helped me put things back in to perspective. I couldn't let the shortest date in history let me spiral to complete despair. By the time I got back to the holy ground of the East Side, she had me laughing at the ridiculousness of my dating life. I decided if nothing else, I had to find the humor otherwise I would be left to cry, and I was NOT going to succumb to that nonsense.

At the sake of sounding cheesy and slightly modifying a terrific quote from Tom Hanks in the film a League Of Their Own, "There's no crying! There's no crying in bad dating!"

Frog #11

"Mr. New Year's Eve"

Every year, my friends and I went to one of those all-inclusive New Year's Eve parties in the city. Someone would organize it and somehow the entire Adult 25-35 population living in Manhattan also managed to receive an invite. All your money had to be in on time or the price would go up and/or you would get shut out because you were the 1,001st person to respond, exceeding the 1,000-person limit. And of course all of this needed to be decided by October or you were left to your apartment with a bottle of Korbel and Dick Clark's Rockin' New Year's Eve as your only viable alternative.

It was the fourth year we were going to this party, so I was an old pro and knew the drill. However, this year many of my once-single friends were now in relationships, so it was a smaller group and I was not as excited as I had been in the past. I think I had out grown making a big deal of NYE (chalk that one up to being a little bit older and wiser). But of course I had a ticket, so I went.

We arrived at the club around 10:30p.m.that night just to make sure we would be able to get food and drinks considering the absurd price we paid to get in. As I had expected, it was a pretty uneventful evening until sometime after midnight, when I met this guy. He was jaw-dropping gorgeous, with an athletic build and had what I referred to my friends as "sexy eyes". I was intrigued; something about him felt mysterious and I was drawn to finding out what it was. I was also on my fifth or sixth vodka tonic.

Twentieth dating lesson learned: Never trust your judgment after your third vodka drink.

Although it was dark and very loud, we attempted to have a conversation while I felt my friends eyeing me from the sidelines. Eventually I gave him my phone number and two days later he called. We made dinner plans to go out for Chinese food.

At first the conversation was going okay, but that soon changed when he did the unthinkable and a definite no-no on a first date… He started to discuss the other dates he had coming up that week! Now call me crazy, but if you are on a date with a girl, what on Earth would make you think she wants to hear about the other dates you have planned for that same week? Is it too much to assume that you do not discuss other dates and plans while on a date? Isn't this just part of the rules of dating? What was it with all of these guys in Manhattan who had missed the basics of dating? Needless to say, this was definitely a huge turn-off.

Strike one.

Strike two came about thirty minutes later as we were just about to order dessert. *Mr. New Year's Eve* decided to share a bit of information about himself that, to be honest, freaked me out quite a bit. He brought up the fact that he often likes to become one with nature and at times finds himself going deep into the woods at Bear Mountain to follow wild animals. He would "follow their poop droppings" and try to guess which animals had left which dropping. That definitely was not a conversation I had ever had on a first date, or a twentieth date for that matter. I was speechless, which 99 percent of the time was pretty hard for me. I could just see a trip up north along the Hudson, complete with us searching to figure out what the animals had been eating for the last few weeks. Just the kind of romantic getaway every woman dreamed about.

Call me skeptical, call me judgmental, call me what you will, but I found his story to be weird. At that point, I passed on dessert, hurried home and crossed him off of my list.

Interlude

"Miss Losing Faith"

After an evening of conversation centered on searching for animal droppings in the woods, I really began to wonder if there were any nice, normal guys left in this great big city. I was being open and trying all avenues of meeting guys, whether it be online, through set ups or meeting them out on my own — and yet I continued to land at ground zero, alone. I started to reflect on all of my friends who were currently in relationships and how easy it seemed for them to have met their matches, their soul mates, and their "person." So WHY was it so hard for me?! What sick joke was being played on me that led me to go on such horrendous dates time and time again? My friends and colleagues kept telling me that when you meet the right one, it's just easy. Things just fall into place and there isn't any of this drama or questioning. I just couldn't imagine it. Never in my wildest dreams would I have thought I could write the stories I had (with more to come), let alone live them myself. I didn't want to become jaded or to lose faith that true love was in my cards, but with each experience, a little bit of hope slowly chipped away.

Frog #12

"Mr. Stuck In The Past"

While I continued to struggle with losing hope that I would ever meet a guy who didn't make me want to run like the wind within the first five minutes of a date, I did still continue to put myself out there. It was a battle on some days, but I knew if I wanted to meet the love of my life, it wasn't going to happen if I hibernated with a tub of ice cream on my couch. So I psyched myself up once again, signed into J-Dork, and stumbled upon the guy that would become *Mr. Stuck in the Past.*

Due to my most recent online dating experiences, I would only allow myself to be cautiously optimistic, when we first started to chat. I fought every urge to let skepticism win over, and allowed myself to feel some level of hope because this guy actually seemed to be normal and cool over email AND on the phone. Now we had to see what he was like in person.

To my pleasant surprise, we actually hit it off right from the start of our first date. The conversation flowed easily and we had a lot in common. While he was much shorter than I typically went for (roughly 5'7 or so), his physique was near perfection and his face easy on the eyes. Being a J-Dork date, it was definitely atypical for me to have been as attracted as I was to him.

We were having a great time as we sipped our vino and shared some appetizers. It was always a good sign when I would order food on a date that started out as just drinks; it meant I wasn't trying to run for the hills after the last drop of alcohol from my first drink had been consumed.

We covered all of the basics — family, friends, work, hobbies, where we grew up — and it became pretty clear our date was turning into something that had potential. We kept the conversation going, and next it turned to where we each went to college. He went to a fairly small school that most people probably had never heard of. But as luck would have it, I had. One of my friends had gone there, so I figured it would be fun to play the name game. I casually asked him "Oh, do you know XX?"

Twenty-first dating lesson learned: Never underestimate the power of the name game.

Unfortunately I didn't get the assumed "Oh My God, YES! So crazy it's such a small world. I LOVE X — she's great!" Instead he lost all color in his face, and looked like he had just seen a ghost. If we were acting on a TV sitcom, the producer would have cued the audio engineer to drop a well-timed record scratch in the background.

As it turned out, his ex-girlfriend was my friend's best friend. I had actually met his ex on numerous occasions. Now, Jewish geography was something I never really understood until I moved to Manhattan. However, I had eventually become very well versed in it, and was completely convinced it should no longer be "Six degrees of Kevin Bacon", but more like "Six degrees of any Jewish single twenty-something."

Twenty-second dating lesson learned: No city is ever big enough — not even one with 10 million people in it.

It immediately became quite clear that this girl had some hold on him. Maybe she had completely broken his heart? Maybe he broke hers? Maybe they just did not have a great break up and hearing my friend's name stirred up bad memories? Whatever the reasoning, there was no doubt I had brought up the ghost of Christmas past!

From that point on, nothing was the same. The chemistry we seemed to have just moments before quickly disappeared and I began to sense his urgency to flee the scene. I actually felt bad for the guy, so I decided to put him out of his misery and ended the date pretty abruptly. Once we made it out of the bar, he could not have walked away from me any faster than he did. It was a total shame this guy was so stuck in the past.

I did hold out hope that he would get over the fact that it was a small world, and the six-degrees of separation (or lack thereof) was not worth worrying about; that he would move on with his life. But, as you may have guessed, I never heard from him again. Apparently, this George Costanza could not deal with our worlds colliding and my short-lived hopes for meeting a normal guy online were squashed once again.

Frog #13

"Mr. Too Much Information"

It was just another day at work until my cousin Ali sent me an excited email announcing that she had just bumped into an old friend of hers. Somehow in the five minutes they were together, she figured out her friend's best guy friend was single —therefore I was obviously now going on a blind date. There were immediate red flags that based on all that I had learned thus far should have been enough for me to know to decline:

1) Ali never met this guy.
2) This all went back to the whole "She's single, he's single, therefore they should date."
3) I had never even heard of my cousin's friend, so why should I believe that she and this guy were even credible?

But against my better judgment, I agreed to meet him. I told myself that I had nothing to lose and really, you just never know. The justification wizard in my mind was working overtime.

Twenty-third dating lesson learned: Never bet against the odds when there is more than one stacked against you.

He called a day or so later to set up a date. I decided since it was a blind date that we should meet at a bar that was a hop, skip, and jump from my apartment. I had learned that lesson and had finally started to apply my own rules to dating. Unfortunately, following these rules meant there were only a few select places to meet these guys. I began to realize this probably meant the bartenders thought I was a complete whore, showing up every other night with a different guy. But at the end of the day, better safe than sorry.

We met one night after work at one of my usual spots. Since I got there first and did not want to appear like that lonely girl sitting alone staring into space, I picked up my phone and pretended to talk to someone (Yes, we do this sometimes). Lucky for me, I did not have to keep the act up long because he walked in two minutes later. To my surprise, he was cute. Maybe this won't be so bad!

Twenty-fourth dating lesson learned: Never judge a book by its cover.

Within minutes, it became obvious that this guy was as dull as my high school economics class. Actually, we were not really having a conversation; it felt more like a job interview. He just kept rattling off question after question after question — I would barely finish answering before the next inquiry came out of his mouth. I am not sure that he was even listening to my answers. I was bored talking about myself.

I kept hearing my friends' voices telling me I needed to be more open-minded. I tried to stay positive and reminded myself that sometimes people were nervous and not always comfortable on a first date.

That theory was tossed out the door when he finally decided to open up about himself. He skipped over the general information I normally like to know — where he grew up, hobbies, siblings, etc. Instead, he began to discuss the always-intriguing ex-girlfriend. I heard all about when they got together, how long they were together, how they lived together, the details of the break up…it was nonstop. Within ten minutes, I felt as though I had lived through their entire relationship. He ended his diatribe with, "We are still great friends because, ya know, she was the first person I had sex with and all."

Um no, I didn't know, but thanks for sharing! I had no idea how to respond. What do you say to that? "Hope it was good?" "Were you her first too?" "Glad you guys can still be friends?" Did he now want me to share my first sexual experience? Were we all supposed to be best friends with the first person we had sex with? He said it as though this was just a fact of life. The whole situation was beyond odd. I wanted to get up and run like the wind. However, since he was a friend of my cousin's friend, I had to maintain some level of politeness. So, as casually as I could, I changed the subject, finished my drink, shook his hand, and sprinted the 25 feet home to the safety of my apartment.

Nice job cuz…

Two years later, my friend from Los Angeles had moved back east and decided to play matchmaker. He desperately wanted to introduce me to his older brother, which of course I was all about, but not before seeing a picture first.

Well thank God Facebook had been born during these single years of mine. When I pulled up a family photo on my friend's page to scope out my latest potential prospect, I realized this brother of my friend's looked all too familiar. As I sat at my computer at work staring at the face looking back at me it finally hit me like a tons of bricks – His brother was *Mr. Too Much Information*! Believe it or not, my dating pool had actually come full circle and I was being set up with the same guy for the second time. Yes, this was what my dating life had come to.

At the sake of sounding like my Jewish grandma, OY VEY!

Frog #14

"Mr. Liar"

It was the start of the summer of 2006 and I decided I needed a little weekend getaway. What better place to visit than Chicago in the summer? So I called Dom, one of my closest friends from college, and invited myself to crash on his couch for the weekend. Given the fact he is gay, I knew I would be spending a majority of my time surrounded by hot men that were more interested in my shoes and new leather jacket than in me, but I also knew I'd likely get my ego boosted in a very different way from this form of the opposite sex. It was just what the Doctor ordered.

However, I will admit that too many nights out in Boystown surrounded by really hot men, and after one too many vodka clubs, I spent a good ten minutes screaming at a group of gay men that "I'm not a lesbian! I'm NOT a lesbian!" I think I started to get confused with all of the testosterone around me and yet I wasn't hit on once. I was quickly brought back to reality when Dom pointed out, "They really don't care if you are. They don't want you!"
Needless to say after that, I realized I had to assume I had no shot in meeting a hot STRAIGHT guy during this trip!

So after a wildly fun but uneventful (as far as my opposite-sex prospects went) weekend in the Windy City, I was looking forward to getting back to New York. I had just sat down in my window seat on the plane, when I noticed the last passenger coming down the aisle. He was so cute and I thought, "What are the odds that this guy is going to sit next to me?" My hopes plummeted when he asked the person in front of me if the seat next to her was taken. Luck or something was on my side because she quickly told him her husband was in the bathroom and the seat was actually not available.

Twenty-fifth dating lesson learned: Never rule out meeting a guy on a plane.

Being one row behind this lady, and sitting next to the only empty seat left on the plane, I was clearly his next (and only) choice! This guy was so good-looking that I could care less that I was the back up.

As I sat there wondering how to begin a conversation with him he introduced himself and we ended up chatting for the rest of the plane ride. I found out early on that he lived in Chicago and was only coming to NYC for business. I was slightly bummed, but if nothing else, he was great eye - candy for the two-and-a-half-hour flight. I was so distracted I hardly noticed the turbulence (which anyone who has ever flown with me would note was quite an accomplishment). As the end of the flight neared, he asked me how I was going to get back in to the city from the airport. I had arranged for a car service, but he offered me a ride with him since he was able to expense it.

It took me less than one second to accept. I was being offered the chance to spend more time with an incredibly sexy, nice guy and not spend a dime. There was no thinking involved in that scenario. It was a no brainer.

Our plane landed on time — 8:00 p.m. on the nose. We got our bags and headed to grab a cab. I could not believe this was all happening — what a great story this was going to be! Little did I know it was about to get better.

As we settled into the cab, he asked me about good restaurants in the city. Completely clueless as to what he was insinuating, I started to make a few suggestions. Halfway through my rambling, he interrupted me and asked if I would like to have dinner with him!

Now I must tell you that I was in sweatpants, a tank top, and flip flops…I could not believe this guy was asking me out looking the way I did. But there was no time to think; he was waiting for an answer. So, after five seconds, I accepted. I decided not to obsess whether he was a rapist or axe murderer, and that I should pursue the "only happens in the movies" situation. Twenty minutes later, suitcases and all, we were seated at a nice table at my favorite restaurant on the Upper East Side. We shared a terrific bottle of wine and enjoyed a great meal. I felt like I had to pinch myself ….was this actually happening to me? By the time we received the check, he asked for my contact information and we agreed to keep in touch. At that point I was still planning to chalk this situation up to being a great story I could not wait to share with my friends. After all, the rational side of me kept reminding the romantic side that he lived in Chicago. It was unlikely that we would actually date. I walked him to the corner so he could hail a cab to his hotel. I hugged him good-bye, and with my rolling suitcase in tow, headed back to my apartment.

Two hours later, he texted to thank me for a great evening and complimented my looks. Although I was flattered and completely thrown off guard, my realistic side was very much present at the time. I did not want to allow myself to get too excited about someone who lived 700 hundred miles away. I just could not ignore that HUGE factor.

Two days later, I received an e-mail from him. One e-mail exchange turned into two, three, and then four. Soon, we were e-mailing all day long for days. In a few of his e-mails, he had started to suggest that I come visit him in Chicago. Eventually, I could not fight it any longer…

I was excited! I could not remember the last time I liked someone. How could I deprive myself just because he lived in another state? There were planes; there were phones, e-mail and text messaging. People dated long-distance all the time — this was not a novel idea. So, after a little coaxing from my friends, I finally threw it out there in one of our e-mail sessions "I'll come to Chicago to visit you. You pick the date and I'll find the flight."

Twenty-sixth dating lesson learned: Do not trust a stranger you meet on a plane.
And then there was nothing. I did not hear from him for days. Was it something I said? Maybe he was just really busy? Maybe my e-mail got lost somewhere in cyberspace? Should I resend it? I was totally confused and wasn't sure what to do.

But like a lot mysteries, give them a few days and eventually they will be solved.

I had taken the day off from work to plan my friend's bridal shower when I decided to check in at work. And there it was, an e-mail from him informing me that he "has a girlfriend who found our e-mails and it has caused problems with them." Excuse me, WHAT?! He had a girlfriend?! And she was upset?! Really?! I can't imagine why?! What a jerk. He then went on to explain that he was just being an "asshole guy and that it was all his fault. He did and said everything he did to feed his ego." He apologized and said it would be best if we did not e-mail anymore because "what was an innocent dinner turned out to be so much more." At least he had the decency to admit that. But not to worry, that was the ONLY bit of credit I would give this guy. The rest of my reaction went like this...

First: NO SHIT we were not going to e-mail anymore asshole!

Second: An innocent dinner? What the hell does that mean?!

Third: God help me if I end up with a guy who goes on a business trip for less than 24 hours and feels compelled to take a random girl he meets on the plane out to dinner, e-mail her non-stop for a week, invite her to come visit, and then call it "innocent" when he got caught!

Fourth: I hope his girlfriend broke up with him for her sake.

And with that, my fairytale romance had ended...I only wish it could have lasted more than a week!

Frog #15

"Mr. Best Friend No. 2"

I am guessing you must be wondering, "Just how many best guy friends does this chick have?" I have always connected with men as friends very well, sometimes more easily than with women. So I have always had a lot of guys that were friends. But once again, *Mr. Best Friend No. 2* raised the question of "Can men and women really be just friends?"

For a very long time with this guy I would have said yes with absolute certainty. And had I ended up getting married in my twenties, I would have and very easily could have stuck to that answer. But as they always say, life doesn't always go the way you believe it will. Or as The Rolling Stones would offer, you can't always get what you want.

Mr. Best Friend No. 2 and I met in college but didn't really become best friends until after we graduated. We both moved to New Jersey, worked in the city and spent nearly every waking minute together. But as I mentioned in the Introduction, at the age of 22, I wasn't looking for a boyfriend. I wanted my freedom and I wanted to just have fun and be independent. I made that very clear, so *Mr. Best Friend No. 2* obliged and never made things uncomfortable. Looking back on it now, we did everything like an old married couple — movies and dinners on the weekends, sometimes going to my mom's together for the whole weekend — but not sleeping in the same bed.

As a typical 22-year-old male, he must have REALLY enjoyed my company because I'm sure there were many sleepless nights there for him. During that period of time, when it came to the idea of intimacy or sex, I did not consider thinking of it from a guy's perspective. I didn't want a relationship, but I wanted to hang out with him 24/7. And back then, what I wanted, I got. Oh how I had begun to long for those days again!

After my now infamous break up with *Mr. Almost But Not Quite Right*, *Mr. Best Friend No. 2* without a doubt stepped up to the plate. We easily fell back into our pattern of spending a lot of time together. In fact, we were together so much my family continued to ask "Why don't the two of you just date? We LOVE him. What is wrong with you?"

What was wrong with me? I was never quite sure how to respond to them or to myself. What I knew was that it just didn't feel "right." There was something missing and I didn't feel this romantic connection to him, which most girls would think I was crazy for saying. He was one of those guys that was pretty much cute to anyone. 5'10, not too skinny but no fat on him, a face that was actually cuter than Matt Damon's, and he always looked great with a tan in the summer. To boot, he was very smart, successful, and to most, a likeable guy. But despite all the wonderful attributes he had to be the ideal mate, something was just "off." So, I kept things VERY platonic, although I must admit I would crash in his bed after crazy drunken nights out with our friends, once again likely causing some sleepless nights for a typical twenty-something male for a long time!

But after years of being badgered by so many as to why I could not just date him, combined with a lot of bad dates, I caved.

Twenty-seventh dating lesson learned: If you know something in your heart to be true and you go against it due to peer/family pressure, you are guaranteed to end up in a bad spot.

During this one particular summer, *Mr. Best Friend No. 2* and I had a Friday-night ritual that included dinner and a movie. We would dissect every aspect of the film, and usually the meal as well. We spoke every day. It felt as though I had a boyfriend with the exception of the one wrench in the whole "arrangement" —He was actually dating a girl we both knew from college. Actually, a more appropriate assessment of the situation was that he was sleeping with her. So while I got to go on the "dates," she had the physical benefit. A definite win for him, but for me not so much.

This went on for about a month when I had my Come to Jesus (or in my case, my Come to Moses) Moment that I had feelings for him. Now, in many cases, this would be an amazing thing: Fall in love with your best friend, get together, and have a really cool story to tell at your wedding rehearsal dinner, just like I had envisioned Harry and Sally had if the credits hadn't rolled as soon as they did in their infamous "When Harry Met Sally" movie.

But this was not the movies'. I had gone a DECADE without having feelings for him. I didn't know what to do with myself. Everything that I thought I knew wasn't making sense. I couldn't figure it out. So I cried. Yes, I cried like a baby. To Marissa, to my mom, I think I even cried to my hair stylist. And they just looked at me like I was nuts and said "So, talk to him." Best friends who were in a relationship since we were practically teenagers and moms who just wanted to see their daughter finally happy in a relationship with a guy she already loved were not exactly the most unbiased of people to turn to. My whole world could come crumbling down. This was my best friend. My safety. My go - to. And now I was going to risk all of that. Didn't they UNDERSTAND?

A month later, he invited me to go to his mom's house in Albany, NY for his birthday. His brother and girlfriend would be there as well which meant *Mr. Best Friend No. 2* and I would be sharing a bed two nights in a row. By now, the sexual tension between us had been building, and we were spending all of our time together. Most people thought we were already dating. I was going to have no choice but to address the "situation" before I really started to lose my mind.

We arrived in Albany for the weekend. Neither of us had said a word about what was palpable enough to cut with a knife. The first night came and went, and I did not sleep a wink. Something had to give. I knew it. I could feel it. So on night two, as we lay next to each other in silence, I was getting up the nerve to say something when all of a sudden I heard

"Court?"

"Yeah?" I responded.

"Um, are we going to talk about the insane sexual tension between us?"

Oh My God. HE brought it up!

So we talked. And talked. And talked some more. You couldn't get two more analytical people than the two of us if you tried. We talked about every possible scenario: "What if we dated and it didn't work out", "What if we didn't date and we never explored what could have been", "What if his ex, who was my friend first, found out?" "What if we hook up and it's bad"… two hours of "what if's" and you would have thought we were trying to solve for world peace that night.

But then finally, after we exhausted every "what if" question there could ever be, we both fell silent, turned to face each other, and started to make out! It felt amazing! Our lips and tongues were in total sync and I wanted the moment to last forever.

Twenty-eighth dating lesson learned: Leave them wanting more. Always.

As hard as I knew this was going to be, I told myself I had to keep this hook up session very PG. After all of the analyzing we did, we had not decided on what we were actually going to do moving forward. Were we going to jump in to dating and a relationship? Were we going to let things play out slowly and see what happened? Were we going to walk away from it all to ensure we could maintain our friendship? None of those impending questions had definitive answers. And if we weren't sure what this was going to be, for my own sanity, I had to be strong and keep the physical activity to a minimum. I was strong in this conviction as we continued to play tonsil hockey UNTIL he said the following eight words to me, "I know everything is going to be okay" and just like that, I was putty in his hand.

The only problem was, being caught up in the romantic aspect of the moment I heard what I wanted to hear which was "Let's do this because everything will be okay." Which is all fine except he didn't say, "Let's do this" … he just said, "everything will be okay." So, I gave in and the next thing I knew we were far from keeping it PG. After all, he was going to be my boyfriend now, right?

The next morning I was on cloud nine. I called Marissa to tell her the amazing news. I was going to be that girl with the really cool story of ending up with her best friend! She was THRILLED for me and for us! She was finally going to be able to put MY dating nightmares behind HER!

Twenty-ninth dating lesson learned: Never underestimate the power of "sleeping on it" and the way sleep (or lack thereof) affects a man's brain.

We stopped by my cousins' house in Albany on our way home. I broke the exciting news to my cousin David and he nearly peed his pants out of excitement. He had always loved *Mr. Best Friend No. 2* and had been rooting for this to happen. I was able to make two people's days and I was floating on air!

After about an hour of eating and catching up, we decided it was time to hit the road to head back to the city. David gave me an extra big squeeze and we left, a happy couple. I was practically skipping to the car. And then, ten feet out of the driveway, BAM! He hit me with "Court, I don't know if I can do this. I'm not sure what I'm capable of. I need time to figure things out."

With that astonishing announcement, we sat in complete silence all the way back home. I should add that the drive from Albany to NYC is three and a half hours on a good day. But just my luck, we were stuck in Sunday summer traffic. I'm sure I'm the envy of every person reading this now.

When we FINALLY arrived at Enterprise to return the car, all I wanted was to flee the scene so I could cry my eyes out. I had held it all in for hours and I felt like I was about to burst. What had I DONE? How far into this was I? Was I going to be okay if he came back to me and said he couldn't do this? Were we going to be okay? Could our friendship survive? A million thoughts were racing through my mind as he tried to rationalize what he meant. "Court, I'm so judgmental. You don't know what I'm like in a relationship. I can be so mean. I don't want to do that to you." Um, okay. So then DON'T!

So much was going on; my emotions were jumping all over the place. The weekend was ending after four hours of the most awkward drive down the Hudson. After our brief discussion and his assertion of how he can be in an actual relationship, he put me in a cab. But before he did, he kissed me on the lips goodbye. Like that wasn't a mixed signal. People who do that are DATING. At that point, on a scale of 1-10, the confusion rating was approximately 1,200. But I got into the cab and soldiered on home.

And that was that.

For the next two weeks, I tried to act "cool." No pressure, no asking what he was thinking. No "What the fuck is going on here." (Though I certainly had those moments!) Just waiting patiently for him to show up at my apartment with flowers saying OF COURSE he can do this. He just needed a little time to digest it. I prayed every night.

Thirtieth dating lesson learned: No matter how hard you pray, you can't make something happen that's not supposed to happen.

A mutual friend was having an end-of-summer barbecue, and we were going together. Well, let me clarify. "Together" as in, our bodies were physically on the same train headed out to the suburbs, but by no means were we together as in a couple dating! While I felt like I was going to explode, I managed to keep my cool and the conversation very surface "How was your week?" "How's work?" "Nice weather we're having"... To anyone other than the two of us, everything was as normal as could be. But for me, I could have used about four Xanax to calm my nerves. Thirty of our closest friends who had no clue what was going on were going to be at the party. Consequently, I was forced to act like everything was the same as always. My parents had discouraged me from pursuing my childhood dream of becoming an actress because they saw how difficult that life was for my sister. I was certain the performance I put on that day was Oscar - worthy. Not one friend asked me if everything was ok or did they sense anything was off between us. My stomach was in knots and my anxiety was through the roof, but I managed to portray myself nothing short of "cool, calm, and collected", giving away not an ounce of what my insides were doing. I doubted many, if any, of our friends would have been too surprised had they known the truth, but I had vowed to him to keep it on the down low until we had it all figured out. Marissa was the only one who knew anything, but luckily she was not at the barbeque; keeping a poker face was not her strong suite.

After the festivities had ended, we jumped on a train and headed back to the city. With about 10 minutes left before we got to Grand Central Station, *Mr. Best Friend No. 2* looked at me and said, "Well, I guess we had better talk about everything." And with that, out it came. "I can't do this. I thought about it. I went back and forth and considered every scenario. I can't do it. I can't do to you what I've done to other girls. I can't do this with you. I thought about showing up at your house and sweeping you off your feet. But I just can't do it."

At that moment, everything just stopped. I wanted to jump off the train. WHERE was the emergency stop cord? WHERE was the conductor? I tried to keep my composure and figure out what the hell was going on but was having trouble even piecing together thoughts to respond. He REALLY had to tell me all of this on a TRAIN? Seriously? This was even worse than the drive from Albany a few weeks earlier. Surrounded by a car full of people, I had no place to go so I just sat there, stared at him in disbelief and said "Well I can't just go back to the way things were". His dumbfounding response was "Why not?"

Honestly, what was wrong with guys? It's like they want what they want when they want it and how they want it. And we were supposed to just go along for whatever ride they took us on. I was really supposed to just go back to hearing about his dates, and telling him about mine? I was really supposed to pretend as though I hadn't imagined what it would be like if we ended up together? I was really supposed to act as though I hadn't prayed every night for the last two weeks that I was going to get to end up with my best friend? Was he serious?

And then the rage set in. I was pissed. ROYALLY PISSED. I was pissed he was such a coward. I was pissed he said everything was going to be okay. I was pissed he was the one who brought everything up. I wanted him to leave me alone, but he wouldn't. He followed me all the way back to my apartment (twelve blocks and two avenues). He tried to hold my hand and comfort me. I threw his hand off me. He was the person I would go to when I was broken. But, HE was the one who broke me! How was this going to work?

I needed time, but I wasn't going to get it. The next weekend we were traveling — together — for a wedding in Breckenridge which meant airplanes, a hotel room, and wedding frivolities for an entire weekend. It was nothing short of a big joke being played on me. I had no choice but to go, suck it up, and put a smile on my face because the weekend was about my friend Nicole and her happiness and not me and my devastation.

To everyone who was at the wedding, everything was just as the way it always was. *Mr. Best Friend No. 2* and I came together and were sharing a room because that is what we always did. No news there. Nothing surprising. All was status quo in their minds. Behind closed doors, it was a whole other story. Any chance we had alone; I wanted to talk about things more. I needed more of an explanation than "I'd be a bad boyfriend." And the more alcohol I drank, the stronger my need for him to explain grew. And the more alcohol he drank, the less interested he was in giving me one. And so it left me with no choice but to once again channel my inner actress and pretend like all was just fine.

On our second full day in the Rockies, and a few hours before the wedding ceremony was to begin, we took a ride to the mountain to go check out the view from the top with two other friends who were not aware of our "situation". Unfortunately for us, only two people were allowed per chair lift, so as we made our way back down, I was paired up with *Mr. Best Friend No. 2.* This would not have been SO horrendous had the ride only lasted the five minutes it was supposed to. Instead, we had the luck of getting stuck about halfway down the mountain for about twenty-five minutes. Just two best friends swinging in the wind, thirty feet high, with nowhere to go and no one else to talk to. I made the rookie mistake of taking the opportunity to start to talk about my feelings about the lovely situation we had gotten ourselves in to. I wanted him to comfort me and make me feel better. After all, that was his job, wasn't it? But all he could muster up was "Court, you are going to have to find someone else to talk to about how you are feeling because it can't be me. I can't handle this." And I couldn't handle his response. I was devastated and so confused by who he was supposed to be to me now. He almost looked different in a way, like he had morphed in to someone else. Someone I didn't know.

I needed a new plan and approach.

I told him that we would get through the weekend, pretend all was fine, and when we got back to Manhattan, I would need time away from him. He was to give me space and that meant no contact – no movies, no dinner, no hanging out, no talking. I had drawn my line in the sand so that I could get my head (hopefully) where it needed to be.

Thirty-first dating lesson learned: When men want what they want, they go from being nice and kind to the most selfish human beings.

His response to my request, "Okay. But HOW long?!"

"I don't know" was all I could tell him. I was being honest, and knew that taking some time apart was going to be the best thing for ME.

The following weekend was Labor Day, which turned out to be a nice three-day weekend to think, think, and THINK some more. I was JUST starting to wrap my head around things when I got back to work that Tuesday and found a present in my inbox — an email from him. REALLY? What part of "I need space" did he not understand? It became abundantly clear he wasn't going to make this easy for me.

And so it went. I'd say I need space. He would give me a day and then reach out. I would cave. We would hang out. And though I really couldn't handle it, I would go along and pretend like I could for his sake and for the sake of our friendship. While he was only half Jewish, he really channeled that side of himself by laying on the guilt as thick as my Mom was capable of. "I can't live in this city without you in my life," he would tell me. He had grown to consider my family to be his "people", and I felt like I was robbing him of the only family he had close by. But unfortunately, with all the worrying I was doing about him, I somehow forgot to worry about me. And that is why you need your best female friend to look out for you. She was the person who has seen you through everything since you were 10; the person who knows you just as well as you know yourself and the person who will be your mirror when you can't be.

Two months in to this back and forth charade, we were all at another mutual friend's engagement party when Marissa pulled me aside and said "The two of you act no different than Dave and I (they were together for six years, about to get engaged). If you don't step away from this and fast, you're going to be in so deep you may not come out." She was right. We acted as though we were together. People who didn't know us assumed we were dating. This was not healthy or normal. The worst part was, he had started to act the way he said he feared he would. He was argumentative, judgmental and downright nasty at times. I realized I was getting the brunt of being in a relationship with him, without even being in a relationship with him. All the negatives with zero benefits. I hardly recognized myself. I needed something to change. And FAST.

So, I did what was one of the hardest things I had to do…. I cut him out. I stopped taking his calls, told him to leave me alone and pretty much acted as though he did not exist. We still had a lot of the same friends, so of course I would see him, but other than a short "hi", I pretty much ignored him any time we found ourselves in the same room. I didn't think I was capable of ever cutting someone out of my life like that, let alone my best friend. But I did it. Despite the pain and heartache, I learned one of the best lessons in life — and it came in handy a lot in the years to follow!

Thirty-second dating lesson learned: It's ok to take care of yourself first, even if you means you hurt someone else in the process.

Eventually I started to date my co-worker (that story is coming) and he was seeing some exotic chick with big boobs. And about six months later, after both of us broke up those relationships off, *Mr. Best Friend No. 2* and I rekindled our friendship. And though years later we are no longer friends, I know for sure it was not because we had taken that risk; the friendship ended for other reasons that had nothing to do with whether or not we had attempted to date. But I can say that the lessons learned from this situation were definitely not in vain and well worth the risk I had taken.

Frog #16

"Mr. Co-worker"

As you learned earlier, for years I refused to date a coworker. I lived by that rule. But as they say, "rules were made to be broken." And I decided it was about time for me to become a rule-breaker.

Mr. Co-worker and I started off as friends. I would vent to him about *Mr. Best Friend No. 2* — ALL DAY LONG. We shared our dating stories and kept each other busy with fun e-mails back and forth, ALL DAY LONG. We complained to each other about work…yes you guessed it…ALL DAY LONG. We had become each other's sounding board. It started with e-mailing one day after our holiday party and went from there. At first, it was purely innocent on my part. I was so messed up from losing *Mr. Best Friend No. 2* that all I wanted was to fill that void. A new work friend was just what I needed and seemed to do the trick!

Thirty-third dating lesson learned: If a man is paying an extra amount of attention to you, he doesn't want to just be your friend.

Sure enough, *Mr. Co-worker* texted me one night to come meet him at a bar a few blocks from my apartment. I thought "Great, I have no plans tonight!" So I picked myself up and headed out to meet him. On the way, I realized we had never been out together socially (other than for a work holiday party which happened once a year). Was this going to be weird? How was I supposed to socialize with someone I usually communicated with behind a computer screen? I started to get a little goosey.

Upon my arrival, I found *Mr. Co-worker* half in the bag, which thankfully helped to relieve some of my angst. Leave it to alcohol to come to the rescue. A few hours later it was just he and I alone in the bar when he offered to walk me home. We got to my apartment and as I went to hug him goodbye, something happened — and the next thing I knew, we were making out. Oops.

Was this really smart? I worked with 40 people, not 400! Did I really want to get involved with this guy? Did I even like him? Was he what I was looking for? Was I that attracted to him? What if people at work found out? A million thoughts going through my head, but for some absurd reason, I didn't listen to a single one of them. I suppose that's what we do when we're rebounding from a bad experience. You don't really think things through. You just want the pain to disappear, so you welcome any sign of comfort or excitement.

And so my secret relationship with *Mr. Co-worker* began. We would meet for "lunch" which really meant sneak to his apartment to hook up. We would meet after work and he would walk me home. Once, we even left work early to go skiing for the weekend. We walked out at around the same time, but met down the street from our building. How people in our office didn't figure out what was going on between us after that move was beyond me. But I think that is what created the appeal and excitement for me. We had this secret thing going on when those around us had no idea. And I will add, watching the guy you are dating give a presentation proved to be a real turn-on for me.

Thirty-fourth dating lesson learned: There is a reason why someone came up with the saying "Don't shit where you sleep."

This secret affair went on for about three months until we hit that point. You know, THAT POINT where the questioning began… "What is this?" "What am I doing?" or even more accurately, "What are WE doing?" "Where is this going? I'm 29, and not getting any younger…" The time had come for me to stare at this and (had I been in my right mind) say, "well that was fun," and walk away. Unfortunately I was not in my right mind. Unfortunately (though at the time it seemed fortunate), good sex had clouded my mind. Unfortunately having someone to go away with, someone to talk to every day, someone giving me attention had clouded my mind. Unfortunately Marissa getting married, comparing myself to her, and once again taking on role as always the bridesmaid, never the bride (think "27 Dresses" and that was me) had clouded my mind. My normally rational mind had become a cloud and one that forgot what she was really looking for. Instead, my clouded mind decided maybe this person WAS whom I should be with. With all of the cloudiness going on, you would have thought I had taken a job as a meteorologist.

The truth was, *Mr. Co-worker* was an emotional pariah, a glass-half-empty kind of person, an angry/bitter at the world type of person, and a person who was NOT looking to get in to a serious relationship. What did this all mean for a girl whose mind was clouded? One word. Disaster.

When I should have walked away at that three-month mark, I started to allow myself to fall for this guy. And really, fall for what? We had pretty much zero in common, came from very different backgrounds, and he had stopped making me laugh. I didn't really even like the guy anymore. But my clouded head couldn't see any of those things and it became all about my ego.

Thirty-fifth dating lesson learned: Allowing your ego to guide your heart is never going to lead anywhere positive.

Eventually the dating part of our relationship fizzled naturally, but I could not walk away entirely, ie: I continued to sleep with him. My attention needing ego was longing for more, especially when alcohol was involved. So I spent the summer drunk texting (and embarrassing drunk texting at that), answering his booty calls, and somewhat longing for what I felt in the very beginning when we had first started dating. It took the entire summer of 2006 for to me realize it was not about him; it was simply about a feeling I wanted to have again. As it often happens with dating, one's head, heart, and ego can get all intertwined with one another and I had made the mistake of allowing my ego to win out for far too long.

It was with that realization that I was finally able to walk away from what had become an unhealthy situation. Why it had to take me a full summer to get the clouds to part and for the sun to start shining again, I don't know. But the time had come for me to reground, refocus and remember what it was I was searching for....

Frog #17

"Mr. Confused"

During the Introduction chapter, I introduced you to Suzanne who had set me up with *Mr. Almost But Not Quite Right*. And, even though a few years had passed, and I had moved on to work for another company, she and I remained very close. She could not figure out how I was still single so she once again took it upon herself to play matchmaker during that same summer I was pulling off that slow, somewhat painful Band-Aid I called "*Mr. Co-worker.*" And while the first set up she orchestrated had inevitably failed, there was no denying she was on target with what I was looking for in the opposite sex. *Mr. Almost But Not Quite Right* had turned in to a legitimate long-term relationship. I trusted she was not going to be one of those people who set me up with a guy just because he was single and I was single so I was actually quite excited about her latest potential prospect. To top that, I had by chance met his parents a few months earlier at her apartment. They were great so I assumed they must have a great son!

Thirty-sixth dating lesson learned: Never make assumptions about a guy based on his parents.

After the basics of the number exchange happened, he called and we set up a date to go out. I was especially excited because I was simultaneously attempting to rid myself from the sex addiction I had to *Mr. Co-worker*. I wanted nothing more than to put that behind me and what better way to find a superior replacement than by going out on a date, right?!

Date one was a ton of fun! We went to a bar in midtown Manhattan for drinks but ended up sharing some appetizers as well because we were together a lot longer than either of us had likely expected. From the second we sat down, the conversation never hit a lull. We had so much to talk about, we seemed to have a lot in common and to top it off I was attracted to him. Standing closer to 5'8 1/2, he was a bit shorter than I usually went for, but he had a very distinguished face with high cheekbones; that mixed with his baby blue eyes and I found I could stare at him for hours. Which was exactly what I did. There was definitely potential for me to actually like this guy and that was certainly a feeling I had not had in quite some time.

Apparently he was feeling the same because he called to ask me out on a second date the next day! He was not even playing the waiting game I had become accustomed to with most of these guys. This was all very new territory for me – a guy I actually thought I could like AND he was doing all of the right things I wanted him to. Miracles could come true.

We met for dinner the following week after work. The momentum we built from our first date increased throughout the night as our conversations grew deeper with more meaning. On date one we had covered all of the superfluous basics of where we grew up, where we went to college, what made us move to NYC, where we worked and what we liked and didn't like about our jobs. But by date two we were on to heavier newsworthy topics including how we viewed the world, what values our parents had instilled in us, what made us laugh, what made us upset, our idiosyncrasies. As we continued to divulge more and more intimate details of who each of us was, I found my attraction to him growing and growing. By the time the bill came, I knew date two had been a success. I sensed it in my gut and it was a great feeling. The stage seemed to be set, and I was excited to see what act was going to come up next.

After we left the restaurant, we walked hand in hand to the subway where I would go Uptown and he Downtown. New York City is interesting like that; nobody gets picked up or dropped off in a car, and your first kiss is not private but usually witnessed by the few hundred other New Yorkers quickly walking by as they scurry to their next destination. And that was fine by me — this was not the first time I was on a date where a first kiss would be in the middle of the streets of Manhattan. As far as I was concerned, it was something I was no longer affected by. I had certainly walked by a make-out scene just as many times as I had put one on. You just went for it with little to no trepidation.

We made our way to the 6 Train (which, for you non-New Yorkers, is the MTA subway train that runs from the Brooklyn Bridge/City Hall to Pelham Bay Park on Manhattan Island's eastern side), and I was looking forward to see how we would part ways. I of course had envisioned a very sensual kiss with the lips he had.

Unfortunately my fantasy did not become a reality.

Instead of a passionate embrace like you would see in the movies, or even just a nice, warm kiss where you could feel a connection with someone, our kiss good-bye was well, quite awkward. And that was being nice. In truth, it was hands down the strangest kiss I had experienced EVER. Now I am not saying you have to play tonsil hockey the first time you make the move in, but there has to be some level of passion and your lips have to be opened somewhat. Otherwise, is it really even kissing?

This guy had his lips pursed and closed together — it was as though kissing me repulsed him. I felt like I was kissing a wall. It was strange, lasted two seconds, and then he was off. I stood on the corner of 28th Street and Park Avenue for a few seconds completely perplexed about what the hell had just happened. Had I misread this guy all night? Was he just not that in to me? I shrugged my shoulders in befuddlement as I made my way across the street to my train entrance, and figured that was it; I would never hear from him again.

Thirty-seventh dating lesson learned: Sometimes guys will actually surprise you in a way you never expected.

After *Mr. Co-Worker* left my apartment in the wee hours of the morning (being physically rejected the night before led me to one of the many booty calls I had made to him that summer), I made my way to work and saw I had mail from my latest date waiting for me in my inbox. He went on about what a great time he had and asked if I would be around that weekend. I was happy for date three to be offered, and yet completely confused. Maybe he was just really nervous? Maybe he liked me but was a private person and was one of the few who actually cared about making out on the street?

I knew these were not questions I would get the answers to unless I saw this guy again so I decided to put away the CIA act and just be psyched I had a date on Saturday night with a guy I thought I liked. When the weekend approached, he agreed to come Uptown. We were going to grab some Chinese food and see a movie. It was a perfect date. And because it was a weekend night, I had hoped I could invite him back to my place and then maybe we could kiss in private!

We met at 7:30 p.m. on the corner of 80th Street and 2nd Avenue. He went straight for a kiss on the lips hello but I was again met with those pursed lips. What was up with this guy? He really must not like public displays of affection.

Dinner was good and the movie was funny, but by now I was not feeling he was attracted to me. Unlike many men, I was a girl who was very in tune with cues and all of his were leading me directly to the way I was thinking. There was not so much as a brush of my arm, a touch of my leg — nothing. So maybe he just wanted to be friends? I wish I could have just come out and asked but I could not bring myself to. I figured at the end of the night he would want to go straight home — alone. And then there would be the answer to all of my questions. I would just have to wait and let it play out.

But as men can often do, he surprised me when he offered to walk me all the way home. The shock continued when I asked him to come upstairs and he accepted. Were we finally getting somewhere?! After an hour in my apartment I realized the answer to that question was no. He was in my little studio until 1 a.m. on a Saturday night and NOTHING. Not one move. Nada. Zip. Zero. Now, I had no intention of sleeping with this guy — But not one kiss?! What was this? What twenty-something guy goes to a girl's apartment late on a Saturday night after a date and does not make one move? I finally decided it was time to send him on his way. I had started to doubt my sexual appeal and I really could not take it anymore. If nothing was going to happen, I honestly just wanted to go to sleep (aka dial *Mr. Co-Worker* and have him make a late night run to the Upper East Side).

I walked him to the door and was once again met with that weird pursed lips kiss good-bye, initiated once again by him. I could not help but think, "Why even bother?" I closed the door behind him and was overwhelmed with complete confusion.

And then it hit me. This guy HAD to be gay.

I stopped for a moment, replayed in my mind what had occurred during the times we had been together, and it was the only explanation that made any bit of sense to me. It had to be he who was actually confused, not I, right?! Of course I did still hear a quiet voice in my head asking myself if I had come up with this theory just to make myself feel better; maybe it really was as simple as he was not attracted to me but enjoyed my company?

After toying with both scenarios for about ten minutes, I decided this was not the sort of challenge that intrigued me. There was the notion that when people play hard to get, it makes the other person more interested. If I was going to be totally honest, this did hold a lot of truth, but only to a certain degree. Whatever game this was, I didn't want to play. I had completely lost interest.

When I woke up the next morning, I decided there was no way I was going out with him again, regardless if he called. Truth was, I really never thought in my wildest dreams that he would, especially after the previous night. But I was wrong; he continued to call, e-mail and text. And I continued to politely decline.

Thirty-eighth dating lesson learned: Always go with your initial gut feeling about a guy because you are most likely dead on

Now comes the ironic part of this whole saga, and the fact that NYC was way smaller than anyone could ever imagine.

I had signed up for a quarter share in a house on Fire Island that same summer. I did not know anyone in my house except the one friend I had done the share with. But our very first night there, I ended up hitting it off with one of the other girls in the house. We bonded by sharing our funny dating stories and what a nightmare it was to date in the City. I started to tell her about my latest experience with *Mr. Confused* and she stopped me mid-sentence. "I know this guy!" she yelled out. "I am a good friend of his ex-girlfriend!"

What?! No way! I did not believe her right away. I mean, what were the odds? But based on my description of the experiences I had had with him — his weird kissing, him not making any moves — she knew who he was, blurted out his name and obvious facts about him, and with that came confirmation.

"Courtney, you know he is gay," so blasé, as if she was telling me the sky was blue.

She said she knew it from the first time she met him. She went on to tell me the only time he would have sex with her friend was when he was coked up. Right. I guess since I did not stash cocaine or any other such drugs in my apartment, he was incapable of even kissing me like a normal human being. At least it explained a lot. Only me!

Two months later, his poor parents who were clearly in the dark about his ways had dinner with Suzanne and her husband and actually asked how it was going between their son and me. She did not have the heart to tell them that he was in fact a homosexual.

Instead she lied and said she had not gotten the latest update. But it did make me wonder… if they were still asking about me long after I had stopped returning his phone calls, was he using me as his "beard?"

One year later, I found out the answer to that question was officially yes. He had finally come out of the closet and I had my proof that it was DEFINITELY he and not I. Validation at its finest.

Frog #18

"Mr. Desperate"

I had been out of the J-Dork world for some time, but after I cut that final tie with *Mr. Co-worker*, Marissa decided she had had enough of my singlehood and was going to take control of my "situation", as she was now referring to it. With that, she resolved the only solution was for me to go out with 25 guys consecutively in order to find "The One."

Her idea was that I would play the part of The Bachelorette (which left her as Chris Harrison) on this dating frenzy. The one exception she refused to really acknowledge was that my choices on J-Dork would be nowhere close to those the girls were given on TV. However, I didn't have a better solution to counter her demands, so instead I caved and agreed to become a dating freak. Marissa's promise to me in all of this was that if her approach did not work, and I did not find "The One," then she would "jump off the bridge with me." Yep, this is what she said. Verbatim. Talk about getting to the root of positive motivation.

And so it began. She would scour J-Date for the men she chose for me, email them, and then get entirely too excited when she received a response. This went on for a few weeks as we counted down from one to twenty-five. While the choices she found for me weren't bad enough to write a chapter in this book, they were also not good enough to write a chapter in this book.

And then I met guy #25; the first of the pack I elected to accept a second date with.

Now if I was being honest with myself, and Marissa for that matter, I knew we had neared the end of this charade she had created for me and I had not made it past date one with anyone else. I knew this was my last shot to not disappoint her, and while my gut told me things would likely go nowhere, #25 was nice enough, the conversation was fine, and I figured I could sit through a meal with him and at least enjoy the company. I even considered the idea that he could end up being a good friend. Maybe through him I would end up meeting new "people". Incidentally, this was the word my mom and grandma often used as code for finding out if I was dating. "Have you met any new people lately?" they would ask. They thought they were so smooth, as if I didn't know the meaning behind the question. It wasn't about whether I had met new "people". The real question behind the question was very simple "Have you met a nice Jewish boy to date yet?"… I digress…

It became quite clear shortly in to the second date that this guy was not on J-Date to meet friends. He had a completely different agenda going on.

Thirty-ninth dating lesson learned: If you know it is not going anywhere, but the guy thinks it is, it's best to cut ties; he isn't taking you to dinner to set you up with the future love of your life.

We went for sushi and just as I was about to bite into the salmon avocado role I had been craving all day, he asked me to put down my chopsticks. While annoyed, as anyone who knows me knows how much I love my salmon avocado rolls, I obliged. He then proceeded to take my hands in his and tell me how great I was and how glad he was to have met me. He went on and on... and on and on… about all of the crazy girls he had met online and that he was just so happy to have finally met someone "normal." Don't get me wrong, all of this was sweet and nice to hear, but it was feeling very over the top. In some ways I did feel bad for this guy. It was clear that he had endured some pretty bad dating experiences, and I was obviously able to relate to that much. However, I was not about to force a romance when it was clear that beyond being able to have a "normal" conversation, we had as much romantic chemistry as you would with a family member. Hopefully no one reading this has any sick and twisted relationships with their family members — if so, then that statement need not apply to you and instead of reading my book, I would strongly suggest getting some therapy. Once again, I digress...

For the rest of the evening, every time I looked up from the delicious sushi I was eating, I found him staring at me as though he were a man completely in love. It had become extremely uncomfortable. There was nowhere else for me to look or go. He would not stop with how fortunate he finally felt to have met me and how great everything was going to be now. It was way too much and I was actually getting nervous that he was going to propose right there and then! This guy barely knew me, other than the fact that I was capable of having good conversation and that I enjoyed eating sushi with chopsticks — and yet he was ready to jump right in to a relationship with me. Everything about this was really wrong.

I had to do something to end this evening sooner rather than later. So, I did what most guys probably fear a lot of girls have done to them — I faked not feeling well. Yep, I sacrificed finishing some of the best sushi I had eaten in quite some time, deciding instead to complain about a terrible headache and stomachache that had somehow concurrently set in out of nowhere. He felt so bad that we quickly got the check and were out the door within five minutes. Nice! Pat on the back for me.

Fortieth dating lesson learned: While I was better at acting than I thought, never under-estimate the persistence of a man "in love".

I was all ready to quickly thank him and be on my way when he insisted on walking me home. He chose to brush over the fact that I said I would be perfectly fine on my own, proving my long time theory that men truly have selective hearing. All cues – verbal or physical – are completely lost on them, and *Mr. Desperate* was clearly no exception to his species. So with that, we were walking side-by-side back to my apartment.

As we turned the corner onto my street, I had a sudden flash of guilt sweep over me. He was a nice guy. Was that not what I was looking for? Was I being too harsh?

By the time we arrived at my apartment, I was reminded of exactly why I had lied to begin with. As I went in for a hug good-bye, he once again ignored my physical cue and instead grabbed my face in his hands. Within what felt like a millisecond, giving me no time to respond or pull away, his tongue was down my throat.

This was a first for me. I had never actually kissed someone where I felt as though I was not part of my own body. While my tongue was raped, I felt like there was nothing I could do to stop it. If the kiss had lasted one second longer I may have actually gotten sick in his mouth. Lucky for him, he avoided the taste of my puke, BUT almost got a good splatter on his shirt when he continued to hold my head in his hands and smile lovingly at me. As my nausea grew worse, it dawned on me. This guy was literally having a relationship all by himself. It was the oddest experience I had ever had.

When I was finally able to get out of his grasp, I ran upstairs and brushed my teeth before even putting my bag down. The next few weeks were spent screening his calls, until I finally came to the conclusion he was not going to stop. I realized I was actually going to have to officially break up with this guy. Yep, after just two dates, I had to have "The Talk." It went something like this:

Me: "Mr. Desperate, you are a kind and nice person. I really appreciated spending a little time with you and getting to know you. Unfortunately, I just don't feel the same way you do."

Silence.

Me: "Hello? Are you there?"

Him: "Yes, I'm here. I just don't understand."

Me: "Ok well I'm not sure what else to say. I am just trying to be honest in terms of where I stand. I do wish you all the best but I am not interested in going out with you again."

Him: "I don't understand. Why?"

Me: "Mr. Desperate, there often isn't always an explanation as to why, other than we went out 2 times and I was not feeling the romantic chemistry. Again, I wish you all the best."

Again, silence.

Me: "Ok well I have to get going."

Him: "Fine. Bye."

Yeah, he did not take it so well. And with that, Marissa and I were one step closer to the edge of that bridge…

Frog #19

"Mr. Stalker"

I have to start this chapter off with a very straightforward statement: *Mr. Stalker* was the reason I took a long break from J-Dork. I was done with this guy before I even met him. It sort of reminded me of the scene in the movie Swingers when John Favreau's character called the girl so many times that the whole "relationship" ended on an answering machine before it even started. Unfortunately I had no idea that this was actually possible in real life…until it happened to me.

I had been communicating with *Mr. Stalker* via e-mail maybe a handful of times before I gave him my cell. I don't really believe in beating around the bush. Give the guy your number, meet, see if there is a connection and go from there or move on. It had become as simple as that for me. And of course, with the proverbial clock always ticking, this approach made the most sense. Why waste time and play games…after all, that was the point of this, wasn't it? To find the right person for each of us and if it was not the current person I was talking to, I had to move on immediately.

I told *Mr. Stalker* that I would only be around sporadically over the weekend as it was Rosh Hashanah. He could call but if we didn't connect, I would be in touch after the holiday. He called that Friday night but I missed it as I was helping my mom set up; by the time I had gotten his voicemail, I was tired and ready for bed.

Just as I started to get cozy under the covers, my cell rang. I don't think you have to guess who it was. I didn't answer and he didn't leave a message this time. OK, a little "stalker like" but whatever. I was too tired to read in to it.

The next day I had to run to the store to buy a present for my cousins' baby (the whole family was coming down from Albany to New Jersey). Just as I was struggling to somehow carry the various presents I had picked out and couldn't choose from, my phone rang. I thought it might be my Mom calling to see if I could pick something up for her, so I dropped all of the toys on the ground and looked to see who it was. It was not my Mom. It was this guy AGAIN.

I ignored his call as I was now on the ground scrambling to pick up the ten things I had just dropped all over the aisle. I had no time to talk to this guy right now. Besides, he had left me a message already. Hadn't I explained I was with my family this weekend? Hadn't I made it clear if we didn't connect over the weekend I would be in touch when I was back in the city? I was starting to get irritated. Parts of me wanted to text him and say, "RELAX!" Instead, I decided to hold out all communication. As his punishment for not listening to me, he would now have to wait to hear from me until Sunday.

I got back to my Mom's with some time to kill before everyone arrived so I checked my e-mail. And there they were — not one but TWO e-mails from *Mr. Stalker*. That made three phone calls and two e-mails in less than 24 hours. I decided to e-mail him back with the sole intention of being honest with him. I had to tell him that he was being too aggressive and it was a bit much for me. When it came to dating, honesty had become my best policy.

What should not have been a shock, I received a novel back within minutes explaining his motives and that he was not "weird or anything". Against my better judgment, I gave him the benefit of the doubt regardless if my gut told me to delete the email, and him, all together. When it came to my dating saga, I had become Jekyll and Hyde. I struggled so much with feeling the need to give my dates a chance versus trusting what I knew to be true. I had heard countless stories from friends like, "I didn't even like my husband when I first met him" or "I thought he was annoying" or "He had some weird tick" or "He talked too much" and "NOW look at us!"

I found myself in this vicious cycle of torturing myself just so that I could turn around and say to all of them, "See, I told you so. I told you this guy wasn't for me!" In hindsight, it was absolutely not worth it; the reward of "sticking it to them" did not outweigh all the time I ended up wasting. It was just hard to see that in real time.

So with all of that in mind, I wrote him back and told him I would call him on Sunday when I got back in to the city, hoping to have finally ceased all communication until then. But as we all could guess, that would have been way too easy. Instead, I was met with an email whose subject line read "Bedtime note for you..." No joke. This guy was incapable of just leaving it alone. And "note" was certainly an understatement; the subject line should have read "Bedtime NOVEL for you". I clicked to open it, took one look at the length, and immediately deleted it. I was still attempting to give this guy a chance and knew if I read his verbal diarrhea, I was likely going to have no choice but to walk away. The fact I felt that way should have led me directly down that road, but I was still taking the measures deemed necessary to avoid a premature bug out on my end.

As Sunday night rolled around, I was finding the idea of calling him to be excruciatingly painful. While I hate to not follow through on a promise, I was completely dreading the call. In the end, I inevitably did the right thing but I found myself on the other end of an extremely awkward conversation that included a lot of dull silences and me straining to get answers to questions. While the writing was clearly on the wall after we hung up, the final nail in the coffin occurred five minutes later when I received the following email:

> *"Hi Courtney,*
>
> *I know you are probably saying to yourself, I just spoke to him on the phone and now he is writing me :o). I know our conversation tonight wasn't exactly free flowing which by no*

means should be interpreted as I was bored being on the phone with you, I don't know if that feeling was mutual on your end? I think the first few times you start talking to somebody (especially sight unseen) are a little bit awkward for anybody/everybody, and for obvious reasons, the only foundation you have is what you filled out on a standardized JDate profile. I think the more you talk, the more you learn, the easier the conversation flows. Personally I feel I am at my best when I eventually meet somebody face to face. I don't know if the same is true for you?

Anyhow, as you have pointed out, I tend to write looooong e-mails so I am wrapping up here, I just wanted to write in case you thought I had reached my peak as conversationalist tonight :o) :o). Have a good Monday....and I'll catch up with you during the week."

I did not know what lessons I was supposed to have learned from this experience. But what I did know was I was not getting paid a dime to be part of this "it could only be true in a movie" situation. And for that reason, I chose to act the part of Houdini and quietly disappeared from his life.

Roll the credits. The End.

Frog #20

"Mr. Picky"

It was the spring of 2007 and after that last stalking episode I had pulled back from engaging with the opposite sex. Unfortunately this self-imposed hiatus had also placed me in a dating lull. Part of it certainly was my own doing, but I also happened to be working really hard, long hours and did not have the time to sign online or even go out all that much. Instead I had to rely on the good old set up to get back on the "dating wagon."

Marissa, who was honestly more desperate for me to find a boyfriend than I was, was on a mission. She had begun to ask random girls in her Pilate's class if they knew anyone to set me up with. She went as far as going to a bridal shower and pimped me out to anyone she did not know. "Hi. I am Marissa. Do you have ANY single guy friends I can set my best friend up with?" She would call me with these stories —obviously with great intentions — and I would feel nothing short of pathetic over what my dating life had come to.

One afternoon she called and left a voicemail that she was setting me up with her friend's cousin. She had the same excitement in her voice as she did when she called to tell me she was engaged. So I felt compelled to call back with the same level of enthusiasm, merely to avoid the lecture that I "had become jaded." In truth, with five-plus years of failed attempts and experiences under my wings, it was hard for me to get really excited about a set-up. I had not given up on finding what I wanted, but had simply given up on getting prematurely enthusiastic about a date. Marissa was still more easily excited so I indulged for her sake. Net/Net: There was no way I was not going on this date. So the whole phone number exchange happened and we were set to meet up the following Friday.

Forty-first dating lesson learned: Your married friends may often feel more disappointed than you are about you not being in a relationship, leaving you to console them. And that's not a good thing. Ever.

Marissa called me the morning of the big day and was so ecstatic. She said she had met this guy once before and thought he seemed really great, talking him up ahead of our evening together. Apparently she had talked to her friend as well, and they had already decided how great this would be if it all worked out. She sounded like a giddy schoolgirl — which incidentally was not making me any more excited. I was trying to play along but it was hard: I knew by now not to put too much weight on a blind date. She could sense my attitude about what I am sure in her mind was going to be a magical first rendezvous, and proceeded to get irritated with me. With my skeptical outlook toward dating, she assured me, I was never going to find someone.

Forty-second dating lesson learned: Those who were in relationships since their early twenties may never understand your skepticism. Accept it. You know the truth because you have lived it.

I had been working late hours all week. Well actually, screw that — it was all month. I was exhausted and drained. It required some significant effort on Friday nights to get motivated and go out instead of collapsing on my couch after I finally made it home. However, I knew that I needed to socialize again before I forgot how. So I went home that evening, took a shower, put on my favorite pair of jeans, and got myself pumped up for this date. I even played some Bon Jovi (loudly) and rocked out in my apartment to get myself psyched up. (Yes for all of you men out there, women do this).

I decided to meet this guy at the same old standby I met most of my first dates (especially when they left it up to me to pick a place). It was close to my apartment and made it easy to escape home quickly if necessary. When he walked in, I was sort of surprised to see he was shorter than I had envisioned (or was told) and had really bad teeth (think Hugh Grant). But he was not the worst looking guy either with his short dark hair, dark eyes, and chiseled face, I could not say he was ugly by any means. While I did not want to jump him at first sight, I could stand to look at him without cringing. With all the experiences I had now had under my belt, this had to be put in the positive box.

Shortly after we sat down we ordered some food and drinks, and the night was off to a decent start. We talked a lot about the blind date 101 basics — where we grew up, where we went to school, our jobs and our dating experiences in this city. We shared our nightmare stories; knowing that other people had similar experiences always felt comforting to me, as though I was not alone. Plus those types of discussion always helped break the ice on a blind date because one person always ended up laughing at whatever absurd story the other told.

While there was nothing about this guy that was really drawing me to him, he seemed to be normal and nice, so I figured I should give our evening together a fair chance. There had been plenty of times I wanted to leave a date after five minutes, so the fact that I was on to my second drink and halfway through my appetizers without losing my mind was a good sign.

By the end of the night, we were making fun of some of the strange people that were sitting near us. The comfort level had grown over the course of the evening, and I don't know if it was the pitcher of sangria I had just finished or the fact that he was the most normal guy I had met in a long time, he suddenly became slightly more attractive to me. I was by no means a woman in love, but I had decided I would go out with him again if he asked.

However, no matter what kind of a time I was having, 2.5 hours in and I was tired. And not, "I'm tired because I'm bored and I have to get out of here" tired, but legitimately "My butt is drained from the ridiculously long work week" tired. Averaging four hours of sleep all week had not been good for this 30-year-old girl. I was ready for bed.

I went on to explain my whole week to him and how crazy work had been. I admittedly let out a few yawns but given my week, I thought it was excusable, even if it was a first date. He said he completely understood and we asked for the check.

Forty-third dating lesson learned: Sometimes when a guy says he understands, he doesn't.

A few minutes later we were saying our good-byes on the street corner. I didn't feel enough of an attraction to him just yet for us to actually kiss. It was not that kind of a date. But I had ranked it a six on my dating scale: Good conversation that flowed with ease all the way through the last sip of alcohol constituted an above average date, regardless if I wanted to jump his bones or not.

I went home and called Marissa immediately since I knew she was waiting anxiously by her phone. I knew this because this is what my married friends' lives had become — living vicariously through me — falling asleep with the phone in their hands so that when I called to report how my dates went they would not miss a beat. I obviously didn't want to disappoint, or worse, not call and incur their wrath the next day for failing to contact them immediately with all of the details.

When I told her it was definitely not the best date of my life but that I would go out with him again if he called, she sounded a bit defeated — even a bit irritated with me for not sounding more enthused. It was as if it was my fault the date was "only a six". I knew this was all coming from a good place – she just wanted me to be happy and that meant having a much more animated tone than the one I had called her with that evening. I wasn't capable of faking it, even for her sake. And at the end of the day I wasn't saying I wouldn't go out with him again, it just was far from love at first site.

Two days later she called me while I was at work to tell me she had gotten "feedback" from her friend. Apparently there was not going to be a second date. The reason why nearly made me fall out of my chair at work, "You yawned during your date and he said he could not go out with a girl who was that disinterested that she would yawn on a date."

Was this guy SERIOUS?!

Had I not prefaced to him that I had worked crazy hours and Friday nights were tough for me — to which he had agreed? Had I not apologized the two or maybe three times I did yawn, explaining that it had been a rough couple of months for me on the work front? I didn't realize how intolerant human beings could be of one another that a yawn would be this much of a turn off. Not that I wasn't cute (which he said I was) or well rounded and grounded (which he said I was). I was amazed. But best of all, so was Marissa. She felt defeated but for once, not because of me. She finally started to see what I was dealing with.

I know that Hollywood wanted us to all believe that you were supposed to take one look at a person, talk with them for five minutes and then hours later the two of you were getting married on an island in the Pacific. Reality was a little different. If a date was going well enough that you could sit through an entire meal without wanting to poke your eyes out with a pencil, it was really hard to tell right then and there if the person you were out with was someone you could eventually spend more time with. Based on that, I believed I needed to see a guy at least one or two more times passed a first date to get a better sense of who he really was and if I found myself capable of actually dating him or if it wasn't meant to be.

Apparently this latest 34-year-old guy did not agree with my belief system. The fact that I was willing to go out with this guy again and he didn't want me because I yawned actually just made me laugh. I do not say this a lot since I am not a cocky person, but the fact of the matter was, I was way out of his league.

In the end, the experience proved to be somewhat therapeutic for me. I realized that I actually was less jaded than I initially believed and that there was hope for me on the dating front. I had become able and willing to give people a chance, and this guy was likely going to be alone for the rest of his life.

So while another one bit the dust, I found comfort in knowing I was the one who was open … and that was what was going to lead me to finding what I was looking for.

Frog #21

"Mr. Sparks"

Although I had gone on hiatus from J-Dorking (thanks *to Mr. Stalker*), I was not ready to completely write-off online dating, so I signed up for Match.com later the summer of 2007 after work had finally calmed down a bit.

Within two days I was bombarded with emails, but only one in particular stood out. It was thoughtfully written, no spelling errors, and included some humor. It was "normal" in every sense of the word. While this guy did not have a photo (which was typically against my online dating rules) something about his e-mail told me I should respond to him. So I did.

It turned out he was a teacher and left his photos off for privacy reasons. Within minutes of asking, he sent a few and it was clear he was a very handsome guy. We exchanged phone numbers almost immediately and he called a day or so later. Our conversation flowed well and we talked about almost everything right from the get go, including our careers. Being a teacher also meant he worked at a summer camp to keep busy over the summer and coincidentally it was the same summer camp I went to from the time I was six until I was thirteen AND I was a counselor at when I was nineteen and twenty. After the next obvious step of playing the name game, we realized we knew some people in common. Not always the case when meeting someone online so I thought this was great and he agreed! It all felt a little less sketchy and I was excited, especially because this meant I could do a reference check before even meeting him.

After I did my digging and found out he was a "great guy", I made plans with him for that following weekend. He lived in New City (a NY suburb outside of Manhattan, just north of NJ) but had no problem driving in so I could stay on my turf. We went to one of my favorite neighborhood spots and spent the next seven hours talking, laughing and getting to know each other. It was hands down the best first date I had had in at least a year. And luck being on my side, he asked me out again that very night for the following weekend. I was actually going to be in New Jersey so it would be easier on him this time around and promised to "plan an evening of fun."

The week leading up to our second date was filled with a lot of text messaging, e-mails, and IM's back and forth (all initiated by him). After just one date it did seem a bit much — especially when he wrote texts that read, "I am going to make you watch re-runs of Lost all summer. It's the best show ever." Considering we had spent less than a full day of our adult lives together, insinuating that we would be hanging out all summer watching certain TV shows was definitely feeling like it could be jumping the gun a bit. BUT I decided I did not want to approach this situation in my typical fashion — he seemed like a great guy so I told myself to relax and just go with it. When was the last time I could spend seven hours with the same guy on a first date?!

On the Friday I was set to head out to New Jersey, my new guy offered to come pick me up at the ferry, which incidentally was WAY out of his way. While it was a very sweet gesture, I declined and opted to grab a ride from my cousin. It did feel like something a boyfriend would have done and I did not want to get that idea in my head yet — not after just one date!

Instead we made plans for Saturday night. I drove to his apartment and he had gotten a bottle of Santa Margherita, my favorite white wine, to kick off our evening. We sipped our delicious vino for about an hour and then headed to a really nice restaurant in his area for dinner. The food was great and as he said at the end of the meal, "the company was even better." Date number two was going well.

Next we were headed off to the movies. Now I have to preface this by saying I am someone who, after 10 p.m., cannot sit through a movie without completely passing out. It just isn't in the cards. Any boyfriend I have had in the past can attest to this, which is why I learned to let them pick the movie even if I didn't want to see it. Chances were I was going to be snoring ten minutes in, so why should they have to sit through a two-hour chick flick if I wasn't even going to be awake to watch it.

Anyway, we were in the movie theater and sure enough, I began to nod off a few times. But being the true gentleman he seemed to be, he let me put my head on his shoulder, held my hand and rubbed my leg throughout the entire three-and-a-half-hour movie. I felt some of this was a little forced as I was still in the "getting to know you" phase where hand holding and leg rubbing did not feel natural to me with him just yet, but because I saw potential with him, I went along with it.

At the end of the night we went back to his apartment for a nightcap where he grabbed me just moments after we walked through the door and kissed me, very passionately. He was definitely a good kisser that was for sure! And it was at that point when I did start to feel that kind of excitement that I usually did when "it" was there. However, I was by no means ready to stay over, so at 2:30 a.m., I got back in my car (well, my mom's car) and drove back to Cliffside Park where I was staying for the rest of the weekend. All in all, an eight- or nine-hour second date constituted as a pretty damn good one in my eyes!

As I was leaving his apartment, I mentioned I was around on Monday so we could get together if he would like to. He said he would and that he would call. Now when a guy says he will call, I am one of those people who actually think the guy is going to pick up a telephone and talk to me. Don't say you are going to ring me if you aren't planning to. There was an entire episode on Friends dedicated to this topic. For those of you who are not as in the know about the series and its characters, Chandler Bing didn't call — and neither did this guy.

Forty-fourth dating lesson learned: Never underestimate a man's ability to completely shock you.

Monday came and went and I never heard from him. I was a little confused based on the way our date had ended, and yet my gut was telling me he was not going to call. When I shared the story and my feelings with some of my friends, they thought I was jumping the gun. "Maybe he got caught up with work or had other things going on." They had all sorts of excuses in his defense as to why I had not heard from him. But I knew. They could call me crazy all they wanted, but when you have a gut feeling, you should never try to convince yourself otherwise.

Forty-fifth dating lesson learned: When asking advice about dating, do not go to your married friends who have been with their husbands since the Stone Age. They will call you crazy and yet you will feel like you just continuously prove them wrong.

When I got back to work on Tuesday, I saw he signed online. Because he had insisted on instant messaging me nonstop the week before, he was obviously one of my "buddies" and now I would know when he was online and when he was not. Ah, wasn't technology great? It gave people the ability to stalk someone, without it really being the act of a crazy person. In essence, it's the electronic equivalent of you being in a somewhat crowded room or bar, and you see someone you know from across the way. So I did what anybody probably would in that situation — especially someone I had gone out on a couple of dates with and who shared with me just a few days earlier that I was going to have to watch every single episode of Lost with him over the summer — I said hi.

He wrote back, but I could tell from the message that he was aloof. While he was proving my gut feelings were correct, I was still completely confused. How does one go from non-stop texting and IM'ing, from offering to pick me up at the ferry, to a great second date, to NOTHING?! I just didn't get it.

And because I did not get it, I did what most women often do: I began to over-analyze everything!

Was it because I fell asleep during the movie? Was it because he did not like my glasses (I had put them on because my contacts were bothering me)? Was it something I said? For the next three days I asked myself these questions — replaying every second of Saturday night in my head. For the life of me, I could not figure it out. He was touchy feely, we had made out — we spent nine hours together for God's sake!

By Friday I could not take it anymore. And against all policies I had ever created for myself, I broke down, and e-mailed him. I made it light and somewhat funny, starting off by saying "I bet you are wondering when I am going to get the picture. Don't worry — I have…" And then I flat out asked him what had happened. How could he go from being so in to me the week before to not even calling the following week? And then I waited for his response…

And waited, and waited. And waited some more. Ugh.

That, unfortunately, was the downside to modern day technology such as e-mail, IM and, texting. The person does not have to answer — EVER. After you hit send, you spend the next few hours reading and re-reading what you had sent, questioning everything you had initially believed was the right thing to write:

"Should I have said it differently?"

"Oh God, why did I write THAT?"

"Did I sound psycho?"

The examples were endless. Until you get a notification that you've got mail, or you see your IM blinking with a new message, you are on edge.

And that was exactly where I sat until finally at 4p.m., four hours after I had hit that "send" button, I received an email from him. And it was from his response that I named him *Mr. Sparks*.

While I appreciated he took the time to write me back, I found what he had to say to be almost comical. He went on and on about how sorry he was that he had not been in touch. That "although you are beautiful, smart, funny, grounded, and Jewish to boot" (yes folks, he actually wrote that), he "did not feel that extra spark he was hoping to find." I was to "believe him when he said he was so disappointed this didn't work out." Huh? What "didn't work out?" We never even got started on something to have it not work out!

After the initial disappointment I felt when I realized I had not actually found a great guy, I started to laugh — hysterically and uncontrollably. I mean, how does a person go from being SOOO in to someone else that it almost freaks the other person out one week to nothing the very next? He had clearly built me up in his head to be someone I either was not, or maybe I was but he had not given himself the chance to find out. The whole situation was very bizarre to me since he was the one who had initiated it all — the kissing, the handholding, and the making plans for the summer. Apparently he was expecting fireworks and the sound of music to play in our ears during our first kiss.

I was not sure what he expected to happen on that second date but whatever it was, there was no way I had given it to him. What he seemed to be looking for was what so often gets played out on the silver screen, so maybe a move to Hollywood would help him find that. But God knows it wasn't going to come from me after 16 hours. So with that... Good luck to you *Mr. Sparks*... and good riddance!

Frog #22

"Mr. Twenty-Five-Year Old"

I, like everyone, had often heard the saying "Ask and you shall receive." Unfortunately, there is also a caveat that sometimes can accompany that piece of advice...

Forty-sixth dating lesson learned: Sometimes you need to be careful of what you wish for.

I had grown weary of all the guys my own age and older. After a long conversation with a few of my other 30 something single girlfriends, we came to the conclusion that we missed the guys that did not have baggage. Those guys that did not have commitment issues or who weren't scorned by the twenty other girls they had met before us; the guys that weren't afraid to wear their hearts on their sleeves and chase after us. Where were those guys? Unfortunately, we realized the last time we experienced guys like that, we were in high school and college.

What a horrible realization. We took a moment to mourn.

With the recognition of that realization, we began to explore what to us was the next best option — we decided we would just have to consider younger guys. If they were 24 or 25, chances were they had not been burned just yet. There was a possibility that they did not have a crazy girlfriend who put so much pressure on them to get married that they freaked and swore off women. Maybe — just MAYBE — this was the answer, and so it became my new theory to dating. I was not yet sure what I was going to do with it, but I felt I was on to something and I was going to have to find a way to explore it.

As luck would have it, a week later I went to a friend's birthday party in Midtown. Needless to say, I was drunk — I mean seeing double, partying-my-ass-off drunk. I went to the bar to get my-not-sure-what-number drink (which of course was totally unnecessary) when I turned to my left and made eye contact with a very cute guy. We started talking about God knows what, as I was surprised I could even formulate sentences at that point in the evening. And the next thing you know, we were fully making out in the bar. Yes, I was THAT girl, 30 years old and THAT girl. Not a care in the world that the majority of the people in the bar were now watching us. There were zero attempts on either of our parts to find a corner that would have provided some level of privacy. Instead we decided to rock it out, or I suppose the alcohol decided for me, right in the center of the bar for the whole crowd to see. We ended up hanging out until God knows what hour and I gave him my number before I stumbled my way home. Sure enough, he called me the next day and it was during our conversation that I found out he was 25. That's right, 25. I could not believe I had discussed finding a younger man just days before and then there he showed up, practically handed to me on a silver platter. Was it really going to be that easy? Was I going to get to date a younger, no baggage man?

I would soon find out the answer.

I had apparently made quite an impression on him because during our second phone conversation he invited me to go to his cousin's big birthday bash the following weekend, where incidentally his ENTIRE family would be attending.

WHAT?! Was this guy for real? While very flattering, talk about going from zero to sixty in seconds!

I'm sure you must be thinking, "What on earth does this girl want? She says she wants no games, she says she wants someone who wants her and chases her and yet here is this cute guy who is doing just that and her response is, "WHAT?!"

But let's think about this for a minute — my first date with this guy was going to be him and his whole family? Come on! I could just see being introduced to his mom and she asks how we met, "Well, Mrs. Twenty-Five Year Old's Mom, I was three sheets to the wind and your son is cute, so I went for it." There was no way this was going to go well. Instead, I suggested that he go to dinner with his family and we could meet up after. He didn't love that idea because he wanted me to meet his family. All week he tried the persistent route, but I was not budging. There was absolutely no way I was showing up to that dinner. Not a chance on earth.

The more I said no, the harder he tried and the harder he tried, the more he seemed to have fallen in love. I am not saying that to sound egotistical, but as a very straightforward fact. Not a rational or welcomed fact, but a fact nonetheless. Forget simply meeting his family, he was practically proposing marriage by the time Saturday rolled around. I nearly puked from the insane amount of cheese that came out of his mouth into my ear, "I've never met a girl as beautiful as you – your eyes are dark but they have so much light in them", "It's a crime how sexy you are"; and he started every sentence with "Baby", "Sweetie", or "Honey". Needless to say, I had quickly lost interest. Not only was I not going to this family dinner of his, but also the constant hounding and professions of love had driven me to not want to meet up with him at all.

So I didn't.

Forty-seventh dating lesson learned: Never underestimate the power of a blow off.

The morning after I didn't show up to dinner and turned off my phone so I could sleep in peace, I woke up to twenty texts and five drunk messages from *Mr. Twenty-Five Year Old.* It was complete insanity. I really wanted to delete them all and never ever speak to this guy again, but felt he needed to hear it from an "older" and "wiser" woman about what NOT to do when it came to dating. So I taught him a lesson (or two or three). He was embarrassed, apologized and asked for a second chance. I just couldn't give it to him, but I sure did hope I had prevented him from doing that to anyone else.

And that was my short-lived experience with a younger guy. He may have not have had some of the same baggage as the older guys I had been out with, but he sure had a LOT to learn about dating. And I discovered one thing was for sure, I was not interested in becoming a professional teacher.

Interlude

"Miss Change In Approach"

The definition of insanity is doing the same thing over and over and expecting different results.

While I was far from what I'd call insane, when it came to dating, I started to realize I had been approaching it the same way for years – entirely too seriously. I was about to turn 31, which meant I had spent six years on the same hamster wheel, spinning and spinning and spinning and always ending up in the same spot. At some point it is up to us to make a change for ourselves, no matter how hard or uncomfortable it may feel to do it; it is what growing and evolving as a person is all about.

So I took a little time to reflect because I needed to get in touch with what may have been the root of my failure to find what I claimed I was looking for. And one day it hit me like a ton of bricks… I was no longer having fun. I had put so much focus on the destination that I had completely forgotten to enjoy the journey! I needed to relax, have a little fun with all of it, and that would mean being more open and tolerant (within reason) of the men I would go on future dates with. Not every guy was going to be "The

One", because let's be honest, unless the very next guy I went out with was the man I was meant to spend my life with, then I still had more Frogs to kiss. And I needed to start to enjoy myself a little with it, regardless of where things ended up.

Now came the hard part...

It was one thing to have discovered what I needed to do, but it was an entirely different thing to actually act upon. I knew at first I would have to work at it. But that is anything in life right? If you want to get good at something, if you want to succeed, you have to try and you have to practice and that meant sometimes falling down.

I recalled the very wise words my Father told me during his speech on my Bat Mitzvah day, "Sometimes things in life are hard, but that is when you pick yourself up, dust yourself off, and start all over again."

And that is exactly what I decided it was about time I did...

Frog #23

"Mr. Rude"

The summer of 2008 was an interesting one in that for the first time in a while, I was meeting a lot of guys and even dating a few at the same time. My new approach was in full effect and it was working. Admittedly, I had even caved and re-joined J-Dork so a few prospects had been straight from that site. I went as far as letting go of my past experiences and started with a fresh outlook. The truth was, online dating was the one avenue that provided the most potential for meeting guys. I knew all of my friends, friends of friends, cousin's friends, cousins of friends – the list could go on and on. So whether it was J-Dork, Match, E-Harmony (you name it and I was on it), it was the sites that had become my number one source for meeting those of the opposite sex.

Toward the end of the summer I met a younger guy (but luckily older than 25) on J-Dork. From the very first conversation he and I had, I had a feeling I was going to hate this guy. Yes, I said hate. Why, you ask? Well, during our first phone conversation, he argued with me about the spelling of my middle name. It's Jacqueline. But he insisted it should be spelled "Jacklyn". I told him there were actually a number of different ways of spelling it. He argued that there weren't and yelled in to the phone "Courtney, your middle name is spelled incorrectly!" He was defiant with a nasty undertone. While my initial reaction was to argue back, I took the high road and told him to "Call my mom and take it up with her". That shut him up.

And now I had a decision to make.

I could A) Walk away from him based on this one part of our first phone conversation, OR B) I could put that conversation aside and agree to meet him because the rest of our conversation was not nearly as bad, I shared his interests in travel and sports, and loved the fact he had started his own business working with kids. While my gut was screaming "He's a rude asshole. Run for the hills!" my head reminded me I did not like people making snap judgments about me and I should exercise the same. "Do unto others," right?

In this scenario, my head won the battle and I agreed to meet *Mr. Rude* Labor Day weekend. He lived in New Jersey right by my mom's place where I was going to be, so if nothing else, it was convenient.

The Saturday he was set to pick me up, I felt myself dreading the decision I had made to go out with him, but my conscience kept me in check and I knew I could not bail. Someone must have been looking out for me that evening because when I climbed in to his car and he greeted me, he was not nearly as arrogant or nasty in person. I'm not saying the guy was a gem, but his tone was nowhere near as harsh as it had come across on the phone when he was playing the role of prosecutor in the "Middle Name Case – Courtney vs The State" earlier that week. To boot, I found him to be even more attractive in person than the one picture he posted on his profile. With his tanned skin, high cheek bones (giving him a more distinguished kind of look), hazel eyes, and what appeared to be very soft lips, I was physically drawn to him instantaneously. He also smelled like camp: he worked with kids all day long at a basketball program he ran, so he had that "athletic" scent that completely turned me on.

He took me back to his place where we enjoyed an amazing view of the city skyline on the roof of his apartment building. We drank wine, talked, and he even made dinner. The night ended with us having a hot make out session on his veranda. Needless to say, I was impressed I had a good time and actually had high hopes for our second date.

From a timing perspective, it was unfortunate that I was headed to France for a week and a half; date 2 would have to wait until after my trip. But I knew I liked my new guy because I thought about him DESPITE the hottie I hooked up with while I was away – we'll call him "Mr. Provence", a chapter that would read as follows: "I hooked up with a very sexy guy from San Francisco on my last night in Provence. It was good. It was fun. I enjoyed myself. The End." And now I was looking forward to getting back to the States to see where my potential new relationship was headed.

Forty-eighth dating lesson learned: The three-date rule is a necessity before you can start to see someone's true colors come alive

Had I been smart enough to not have completely dismissed our first phone conversation, I may not have been as shocked as to what transpired on date 2. Unfortunately, I had traded in my good judgment hat for my let loose and have fun hat, leaving any sense I had in my coat closet at home. All of this proved to be an unwise move; I likely needed a hat that combined a touch of both.

On the evening that we were getting together, he showed up at my apartment, offered no hello, no ANYTHING, and instead just stormed in talking on his cell phone, dealing with what was clearly work nonsense. He plopped himself on my couch, put his feet up on the coffee table (without taking off his shoes), and proceeded to yell into his phone for the next ten minutes.

Was this not our SECOND date? What happened to a nice kiss hello and a "How was your trip?" I guess since our first date went so well he felt like we were allowed to act as if we had been dating a year? Actually screw that, I don't care if I was married to you, there was no excuse for anyone to be that rude EVER.

BUT my "relax and have fun" approach stopped me from kicking him out immediately. Instead I took a deep breath, waited for him to hang up the phone, and hoped for an apology; which I eventually got, albeit a mediocre one at best. He did throw in a compliment by saying something like "I love being around you cause you're so cool.

Most girls can't deal with me and you're just so great about the way I am."

Well not really, but I was going to let him think that… for now, anyway.

By our third date I slept with him. It was not what I had initially expected or set out to do, but by that point I knew by his actions, demeanor, and overall character, my hopes for this being anything more than a physical thing had been shattered. I could NEVER take someone like this guy seriously, nor could I ever have feelings for someone like him. While his "softer" side had come through on our first date, it went back in to hiding by our second and I knew halfway through our third, it was likely never going to show up again. And even if it did, it would never be enough for me. So with that, *Miss Change In Approach* took over and I decided, why not get what I could physically and leave it at that? Men did this very thing on a regular basis and I thought why should I not be able to do the same?

Of course he assumed my actions meant I was really in to him. For some reason guys had a hard time wrapping their heads around the notion that just because we wanted something from them physically did not mean we wanted something from them emotionally. Contrary to popular believe, we were able to separate the two and could be physically into a guy without having any feelings for him. But in typical male fashion, this guy could not even fathom that I, or any woman for that matter, could have felt this way. If he had any clue at all, he would have realized there was no way I could have had feelings for a guy like him. The plain truth was, I was staying in it for both the sex and the pure humor I found in knowing he believed I was into him way more than I was.

He added fuel to my fire when we were out one night and he announced, "You know, I really only date older women because I'm more mature and know what women need and want."

WHAT?!

This guy did not have a clue about women nor what they wanted. He was by far the rudest guy I had ever dated and his perception of what dating a woman was about was so far from reality.

As I let out a really hard laugh to his proclamation, he was startled and asked, "What is so funny?"

Well, *Mr. Rude*, where shall I begin?

"I do not know who your mother is, but she clearly did not raise you right. How a 28-year-old guy did not know it was rude to be on the phone every time he either picked up a girl in his car or when he walked in to her apartment is beyond me. The fact you walk 10 feet ahead of me every time I'm carrying three bags and never offer to help is the opposite of a gentleman. It is completely naive of you to think you can call me every 2-3 weeks with the expectation that I would take you seriously! And lastly, you argue about the most insignificant things, which just continues to perpetuate your obvious immaturity not only as a man, but also as a human being. "

I left him completely speechless with my rant. Not only was a crash course in Dating 101 required for this schmuck, but a visit from Miss Manners was evidently required too. I was done. While the sex was nearly the best of my life, I had to give it up. It was just not worth the aggravation and annoyance this guy had started to cause me. I graciously bowed out and walked away.

Forty-ninth dating lesson learned: If a guy is a shmuck, then he's a shmuck. And dating a shmuck, no matter how intense the physical chemistry may be, is nearly impossible.

But as my sister had been telling me for years, no matter what you do, like vampires, they always come back.

While *Mr. Rude* acted unfazed when I ended things, two months later I received a text from a number I did not recognize (I had deleted him from my phone). After a little sleuthing, I was not at all shocked to discover whom it was from. The comical thing to me was that he thought I was actually going to hang out with him and seemed shocked when I politely, but firmly, declined. Two months after that, I received yet another text that warranted the same response from me. You would think after getting a reply that read "I'm not sure who this is…" would have helped him figure out that I had not only deleted his number from my phone, but was also not interested in contacting him. Maybe I should have named him Mr. Clueless.

The following summer, right after I broke up with my boyfriend (oh yeah, getting to that chapter), I received ANOTHER text from him. I will admit that with circumstances being what they were, I was tempted to go for the rebound sex. We have all done it at some point. But after thinking about it for one minute, I realized good sex or not, it was not worth it to go there. This time I did not even bother to reply. He FINALLY got the picture, never to be heard from again.

Frog #24

"Mr. Chicago"

My bout on J-Dork this time around had led me to at least getting past date one and even some hooking up. So I extended my membership and became much more open to possibilities. I even extended those possibilities across state lines…to the Mid-West.

I had received an IM from this guy in Chicago, and my initial reaction was "What am I going to do with a guy in Chicago?" But if I was going to stay true to my new, more "carefree" attitude of having fun, then I could not eliminate any possibilities. His profile picture revealed a more rugged look than I was used to in NY, but it was one that I liked. The NY guys tended to be polished (almost too polished for my liking) and leaned on the preppy side. He had on a t-shirt, jeans, flip flops, and had sunglasses propped on his head in the one photo I had of him. He looked hot in an "I'm not even trying to be" kind of a way that actually made my insides turn in a good way. That mixed in with his cute dimples and what seemed to be a quick-witted personality, I was intrigued. I decided there was no harm in a little flirtatious IM, and in the spirit of keeping the right energy out there; I proceeded to instant message with him. All day.

This guy had me cracking up and even more so, he seemed to get me. I agreed to call him that night and as we spoke on the phone, the intrigue grew. But was I crazy? When did I think I was going to meet this guy? He lived 711 miles away from me.

After only a minute of this thinking, I brushed it aside and kept up a sporadic texting, IM'ing relationship with him for the next two months. At the end of the day, he made me laugh so it was a form of entertainment. When we went a few days without being in touch, he always seemed to cross my mind because I had not had the same interaction with anyone else whom I had met on this site. I had my doubts because most of our communication was done in cyber/texting space, but there was no real harm being done at this point so I kept the fun going.

By mid-November the sporadic outreach started to become frequent, and I found myself (do I dare say it) liking this guy. Could this really be happening? Could I be getting more attached to him than to anyone else I had actually met in person? What was this?

I was off to Florida for a mini-vacation, and he asked that I text him when I landed. We joked about the fact he was treating me like I was his girlfriend. In ANY other situation I would have completely bugged out — this was not normal. But it felt normal so I went with it and texted him when I landed.

My entire Florida trip we were in constant contact — texting non-stop all day, speaking on the phone a few times. By the end of the week, my friend Juliana (who was with me on the trip) said, "You two better meet, because you are actually starting to like this guy and you don't even know him! What are you doing?" I knew she was right. It felt so right and yet it all was such different territory for me. What were we doing?

I decided he should come to New York and we should meet. We had to find out what this was…I couldn't have an E-boyfriend – it was getting weird (at least for me). He agreed.

However, by the Monday before the weekend he was supposedly coming, he still hadn't booked his ticket. Seriously? I wasn't sure what was going on, but that trusty gut of mine was telling me he was not getting on a plane. Maybe it was wrong to assume that, but in truth, I didn't know this guy. I thought I had started to, I had this strange attachment and was drawn to him, but was it real if I had never met him face to face?

And so the IM interrogation began — and it all went wrong.

Fiftieth dating lesson learned: The world of instant messaging, e-mailing and texting leaves an incredible amount of room for interpretation and misunderstanding.

I sent him a message saying I thought it was pretty clear he was not coming to NY because if he was planning to, I would have assumed he would have booked his ticket by now. Needless to say, he did not take what he deemed as an accusation well, and said he now felt a red flag go up for him. This made me very upset. Anyone who knew me knew I was not a red-flag girl. I was open, honest, down to earth, and just said it how it was. Unfortunately, as much as we had these chats, we didn't KNOW each other. And therein was a big part of the problem. This guy was left to interpret all of this any way he wanted to. He knew me through our electronic conversations and occasional phone calls, but he didn't KNOW me like he would if we went out for dinner and I made a smartass comment about a couple at another table, or what things really could irk me.

In the end, we IM'd the next day and he expressed that he was now torn and conflicted about coming to meet me. Given I had accused him of no longer coming, when he never actually said that was the case, had really annoyed him. I was upset, but what could I do? He left it by saying he needed some time to think about things and I said fair enough. He signed off, and unlike *Mr. Rude*, was never to be heard from again.

Once again I was left questioning how a person was capable of going from non-stop communication, to one IM misunderstanding, to radio silence? I let a week go by, and then reached out to him with a phone call. He did not pick up so I ended up leaving a voicemail. I could not just let it go without at least saying what I needed to say, out loud and not via IM. I figured he would not call back but I stayed true to myself. And that was that — I let it go.

Although I couldn't 100 percent let it go. He popped up in my head every so often as I continued on my quest for relationship bliss. I had not had the same interaction with any other guy I had met recently. This was by far the most interesting dating situation I had ever found myself in and yet it was over before it began. I now had to deal with the feelings that came with a break up and I had not even met this guy in person! Only me…

Fifty-first dating lesson learned: Feelings can have a crazy impact in ways you would have never expected they would; it's what makes them the relationship wild card.

Frog #25

"Mr. 180°"

At the point in which I was in my dating career, I learned that although I had my list of criteria, I was not going to get everything on that list. I had been told numerous times by my happily married friends that if I got anywhere between eight and nine on the list of ten, I would have struck gold. And seven was absolutely solid. So when I met my latest online match, and I figured out in the five hours I had spent with him that he had about six of the ten things on my list, I thought maybe — just maybe — this one had potential.

He and I talked about everything you could possibly imagine on that first date. By the end of the night I knew who would be his best man at his wedding, what he wanted to name his first-born son and daughter, and the fact that he had gone to therapy after his aunt died. We shared some very intimate information between us that went well beyond the typical details shared, like where you went to college or how many siblings you had.

For our second date, he offered to take me out for a really nice steak dinner where we were out for close to six hours. By then, I assessed he had seven to eight of the things on my list of ten. However, other than finding him attractive and his ability to be serious, the rest were all hear se based on what he was telling me he was like — adventurous, light-hearted, kind, fun, hard working, and family-oriented. So while I was excited and hopeful, I knew I could not be senseless enough to ignore the simple fact that I had not actually seen him display such characteristics yet.

He spent a good portion of our second date selling me that he had this very lighthearted "don't take life too seriously" side, but thus far I had only seen how intense he could be. While I enjoyed the thoughtful talks we were having in this "getting to know you" process, I wanted to see that "lighter/funnier" side to him. That was part of my criteria — I needed to be able to be really serious and intense with someone, but at the same time have the ability to laugh like crazy and keep things light as well. I was in search of that illusive "perfect" combination.

Fifty-second dating lesson learned: Actions speak louder than words. Just because a guy says he does this or that, does not mean he really does.

So when we made plans for date three to be the Saturday of the following weekend, I was really excited for both of us to let loose and show our more "fun" sides. We spoke on the phone for twenty-five minutes on Tuesday night and decided we would talk later in the week to finalize plans. This was another interesting and great element about this guy…in the world of texting and e-mail, he still picked up the phone and called me. He would check in throughout the week with via text but would often follow up with a phone conversation at night. It was a great combination for me.

However when I had not heard from him by Friday night, I started to get that strange gut feeling — the one that told me things were no longer copasetic. I tried to ignore it, but it was no easy task as I had too much experience to close a blind eye. A few hours later, I decided I would have to take the bull by the horns and test my theory. I reached out via text asking what time worked for him the next night, looking to see if I would get a response. He had been so proactive the week before, picking the "perfect" steak place to take me to, and now we were less than 24 hours away from date three with no set plan made. In a few short days his behavior seemed to have done a 180°.

Three hours went by, and I still had not heard back from him. My mind went straight to two words — Blow Off. I will admit patience was not always my strong suite, and so as I tried to remind myself that three hours was really not that big of a deal, I had a hard time believing it.

Another thirty minutes went by before I received a text that only read "7 p.m.?" I responded that time was fine, but I knew in my heart that something was up. There was no follow up text after I wrote back. No information. No discussion of a plan. No nothing. With it being this early in to things, I was left with nothing than to know this meant something had changed. My friends of course thought I was being completely irrational in my thinking.

Fifty-third dating lesson learned: Do not listen to your friends tell you that you are wrong — your gut reaction was yours to have and own.

The next morning I woke up and knew I was not going to go out with him that night. You can join my friend's bandwagon in thinking I was nuts, but I will swear to this day on my gut always leading me to the truth. I went about my normal routine — spin class, lunch with friends, back home to shower. After all of that I finally looked at my phone for the first time all day and saw the following text from my alleged date, "My aunt got in to a car accident. I'm on my way to Long Island."

I am typically one of the most compassionate people when it comes to tragedy or bad things happening. My current boss would often accuse me of having a bleeding heart. So when my initial reaction was to not believe him, I knew this was never going to work out. There was something inside of me that did not trust this guy. How could I when I saw a green circle indicating he was available on IM just minutes later? If he was really in his car driving to Long Island to see his aunt in the hospital after she supposedly got in to a car accident, how was he on his computer? The guy's aunt could potentially be in critical condition and I had no sympathy whatsoever. Horrible? Maybe. But if he was lying, as I believed he was, the answer to that question was undeniably, NO.

My next move was to promptly make other plans. I am not one to sit around and wait for a guy. In my mind, he had pretty much cancelled

— otherwise why would he have texted me that information. I was going to go out with *Mr. Best Friend #1* and his brothers in Hoboken. That would be a perfect distraction to not feel bad about any of this!

A few hours later, as I put on the finishing touches of my make-up, I had managed to erase *Mr. 180°* from my mind and refocus on having a fun night out with friends. My distraction plan was in full force until I received a text that threw a wrench in things. It was from him asking if I was still available tonight. Ugh!

I say "Ugh" for a few reasons. First, I had made other plans and I did not want to go back on them now just because this guy showed back up. And second, maybe my gut was wrong? Maybe I was losing my touch? Maybe I had jumped the gun too soon in making my back up plans and should have been more patient?

I called Marissa for advice. I told her about my feelings on this; that something just felt off about this whole situation, but I was now second-guessing myself. She told me I needed to get out of my head and go out with him. I had plenty of drunken Hoboken nights out with *Mr. Best Friend #1* under my belt and my time would be better spent figuring out my feelings about this new guy; that I would only be able to really gauge if he had been lying, if we were face to face. So I took her advice, threw all my trepidation out the window and simply texted back "Sure, what are you up for?" To that, I got "Can you get on a train and come down to Manawan."

REALLY dude?! Manawan?!

Before I go on my rampage about Manawan please know I have nothing against the town. To put it in context, it's in New Jersey. I'm from New Jersey; I go there all of the time. However, it was an hour and a half away from the Upper East Side. We had never discussed me going there. This would require me to have the lovely choice of getting on a train at 1 am to come back to the city by myself or to stay overnight in Manawan, which I was nowhere near ready to do. Not to mention, if he had asked me earlier in the week I could have gone out there earlier. Or even yet, if he had called and said, "Look

I've had a really crazy day. I know it's a lot to ask but would you mind coming here? If not, I understand and maybe we can reschedule." Or something to that effect; you get the point where I'm going with this. Instead, this discussion was taking place all over one-liner text messages, five minutes before I was supposed to leave for my new set of plans. Suffice it to say, this was not happening! I was happy when Marissa validated my feelings and agreed with me (I had called her literally after every text because I had no longer trusted my decision making process). She actually thought this whole thing was getting ridiculous. Was justification coming? Was my gut not wrong after all?

She suggested I stop with the texting and just call him.

While it may have been the right move, I did not take her advice right away and instead texted back saying I really didn't want to go to Manawan that night. I offered to meet him halfway in Hoboken and apologized while doing so. Why? I'm not even quite sure other than I felt slightly bad I was so opposed to Manawan when he had had no issue coming to NYC two times already.

However, my guilt quickly diminished when I received a text back that only read "OK, never mind then." That was it? We were not even going to discuss an option to get together? If this was where things were going to end up (and we can't forget I had already had the feeling they would earlier in the day), had he just suggested Manawan because he knew damn well I would never have gone for it? This all started to feel like a big game I had zero interest in playing. So I bit the bullet, took Marissa's advice, and called — no surprise, he did not pick up. I left a nice voicemail. And I never heard from him again. I was bummed for about an hour, and then I was over it and on my way to Hoboken for a fun night out with the boys.

Fifty-fourth dating lesson learned: When a guy avoids the phone call and purely looks to communicate via other electronic means, he is looking for an out.

On September 24, 2009, (9 months later) *Mr. 180°* e-mailed me "Hi, How are you?" Unbelievable…or was it? In the end, it didn't matter. I never responded and simply hit the delete button.

Fifty-fifth dating lesson learned: Men used the reappearance act just as much as they used the disappearance act.

Frog #24 Repeat

"The Impressive Return of Mr. Chicago"

On January 1, 2009, at about 5 a.m. or so — the end of New Year's Eve or the start of New Year's Day, depending on your outlook — I was drunk, surfing around on Facebook when *Mr. Chicago* popped up in my head. I missed our chats, and while I didn't know what it was about him, I had this burning feeling that he was meant to be in my life. So I did what any stupid smashed girl does at 5 a.m. in the morning: I looked him up, and with one drunk click, I requested him as my Facebook friend. This was both the great thing — and the not-so-great thing — about the interconnectivity we have in our world today.

I woke up the next afternoon and remembered what I had done. I was mortified. This guy had disregarded me almost two months ago. What would have made me think he wanted to be my friend on Facebook?

Fifty-sixth dating lesson learned: 99.9% of the time, making decisions when you're drunk will lead to regret. But there was always the chance for that .1% outcome

I signed in to my account that afternoon and to my astonishment, *Mr. Chicago* had clicked his "accept" button. We were officially "Facebook Friends".

His course of action led me to feel the need to address the incident that had occurred between us just two months prior. So I wrote a short e-mail that simply said "Hey Chicago…glad to see after that whole IM debacle a few months ago that we can still be Facebook friends. Happy New Year!" I did not expect anything, but was happy to know that should I ever find myself in Chicago, I did not have an enemy there as I once assumed.

About three weeks later while I was at work, buried in spreadsheets and media budgets, I saw his screen name flashing on the bottom of my computer, indicating he was speaking to me. I enlarged the instant message to find, "Hey, how are you?"

I'm not sure why I was the least bit shocked after all of the lessons I had learned to date about men, but for whatever reason, I was. Never in a million years did I think we would ever speak again — Facebook buddies or not.

Fifty-seventh dating lesson learned: Perception is 99% projection

I paused for a minute and wondered, "Should I open this door again?" I pondered over this question for about ten seconds before I said hi back…

For the next few weeks, he and I talked every day via instant messenger, and then a few times a week on the phone. I was truly enjoying being back in contact with him, had zero idea where or what it would lead to, and didn't really care. I was content.

And then the moment of truth arrived.

Mr. Chicago: "Court, I'm going to be serious here for a minute. Are you sitting down?"

After my heart skipped a beat from his dramatic delivery (I never seemed to know what to expect from this guy), I replied.

"Yes. Why?"

Mr. Chicago: "I really messed up a few months ago. You and I have such great conversations and you are so amazing. I would love to have a second chance, make it up to you, and come to New York City to finally meet you."

Ok pause.

I had two roads I could go down. On the one hand, we could just keep this great banter/talking thing going and leave it at that. I had this great guy who I was able to talk to about anything — but could I just dismiss the fact he had already let me down once before. Did I risk the chance of this going sour again? Should I at least make him sweat it out and work harder for this redemption and chance to come meet me? Or on the other hand, should I venture down the second road, throw caution to the wind, and agree to meet this guy I connected with in a way I had not with anyone else in years (if ever), who I loved talking to, who I felt in many ways I knew so well, and who I actually was excited to meet? Did I just say screw it and go for it because that is what life is about, taking chances?

After a longer deliberation this time (nothing like letting him sit and stare at his computer screen waiting on my response), I chose that second road. Life was too short to play games just to make a point; it was time to roll the dice and go for it. Besides, we had determined one of three things would happen:

1) We would really like each other and have a really fun and enjoyable weekend.
2) We would end up as friends but still have a nice weekend.
3) We would not really like each other and he would leave and go spend the remainder of the weekend with his Aunt in NJ.

All seemed harmless so with that, *Mr. Chicago* booked his plane ticket to New York for the weekend. I was beyond excited!

And so the countdown began.

Mr. Best Friend #1 would e-mail or text every day to remind me of the days left until his arrival. The closer it got, the more and more excited and more and more nervous I got. 85 percent of me knew all was going to be just fine — but there was that 15 percent annoying alter-ego voice in my head telling me otherwise. I hated that voice. I eventually would learn in therapy that I had to name that voice — like a different name than my own. I had chosen "Elphaba" as in "The Wicked Witch of the West" and I had to speak to her like it was a bad friend, essentially telling her to shut up and go away. It was a very interesting technique that when you worked hard enough at, actually worked.

It was February 19, 2009, the day *Mr. Chicago* was arriving. In preparation, I called out sick to work so that I could clean my apartment and get my hair blown out. And let's be honest, there was absolutely no way I was going to be able to sit through an entire day of work with the bundle of nerves I had going on!

At 7:00 p.m. I headed to LaGuardia to meet him and was FREAKING OUT. My head was playing mean, wicked games on me. What the hell was I doing? I don't live in the movies, and this was absolutely a scene right out of one. My mind was running at 10,000 RPMs, and I could not get it to slow down. What if he hates me? What if I hate him? What if I like him and he doesn't like me? What if it's the reverse?

All of the "what ifs" had started to completely overwhelm me. It was not good.

Thank God I have fantastic girlfriends. I called my friend Sam who I had known since we were little tots in the first grade. She was one of those girls who men had always LOVED – she was hardly ever without a boyfriend and while she never revealed her secret to success with the opposite sex, I knew she would provide me with the right advice to deal with my current circumstance. She always seemed to be able to find the "fun" in any situation, and her guidance never fell short.

"It is absolutely imperative you go straight to the sports bar right outside his gate. Order a vodka and club soda and slug it back immediately. This is the only way you will be able to calm you nerves."

I did not argue and did as I was told. And sure enough, the Russian nectar did its thing and I had a slight buzz going right as his plane landed. Five minutes later, my phone vibrated with a text from him that read, "I'm here, no turning back now!"

Vodka in the system or not, my heart made its way to my throat; but what transpired next, I could have never predicted even with the help of a crystal ball.

When I spotted him walking toward me, I felt a sense of calm. And when he was finally standing in front of me, it was as if I knew him my whole life. It felt as though I was picking up my long-term boyfriend at the airport after a VERY LONG — like 31-years long — business trip. It was insane. If I were not there experiencing it myself I would have never believed it. We kissed passionately right there in the middle of the airport and then were off to spend one of the greatest weekends together.

Over the next two days, we would both found ourselves saying things like, "Why does it feel like I've known you my whole life?" and "I can't believe we just met yesterday". What this all meant for the future, I had no idea, but I knew that I had been right to trust my gut feeling from a few months before that this guy was meant to be in my life. During that first weekend we spent together, we went to dinner, walked around the city, watched movies, ate New York pizza, went for brunch — we were a couple in every sense of the word. The way I fit right in to his arms, our amazing physical chemistry, and our conversations continued to be easy and real. There was not one awkward moment within those 72 hours. I could go on a date for an hour and it could feel longer than the time we spent together. It was an amazing few days.

But because I had been living in the moment, when the time came for him to leave on Sunday, I had not prepared myself for the dull, sad feeling that would overcome me. I certainly had not expected all to go as it did. If anything, I had expected I would end the weekend feeling some level of interest in him. I had assumed we would have faced some awkward moments. Or at the very least, we would have gotten on each other's nerves here and there. I had not prepared myself for falling in love. But without a doubt, that was exactly what had happened. It was like nothing I had ever experienced before.

After *Mr. Chicago* left, I called my cousin Ali to tell her about my weekend and all I could say was, "Oh shit… I feel so vulnerable. What am I going to do?"

I quickly realized there was not much I could do. It simply was what it was. I was in…and deep. My heart had been opened up again and as terrifying as that was; I could not run from it.

However, I made a conscious decision to play everything as cool as humanly possible. Doing this was going to be one of my greatest challenges. First, my feelings were my feelings — how and why should I hide them? And second, we were long distance, which meant I was going to naturally feel more vulnerable due to having to go weeks without seeing each other.

About three weeks after his first NYC visit, I went to Chicago for a weekend and had an amazing time. The time we spent together made me realize just how strong our connection was, and the more I got to know him in person, the harder I fell for him. We could literally do anything together — lay on the couch and watch TV, go to a museum, go to dinner, go out on the town, lay around in bed and just talk…hell, I let the man fart on me and I found it endearing. We had great chemistry and incredible sex, and not just because it was good but also because I loved him. We were so natural together and my heart ached the first few hours after I had to leave him.

I did see the bigger picture and had to trust that all of this happened for a reason. Most days everything was great. We continued to instant message every day to stay in constant contact. He kept me laughing, he listened to me bitch about work, we had great banter, and we made a date to take a break from work every day at 3p.m. CST/4p.m. EST to play Family Feud online together. We did everything we possibly could to make the physical separation between us less intrusive.

However, make no mistake — trying to carry on a long-distance relationship was hard. There were times I just wanted to come home after work and have him there to order dinner and cuddle up with on the couch. Unfortunately, all those miles in between meant we did not have that luxury. Instead, we had to rely solely on instant messenger and the phone. And while that afforded us the chance to have a deeper emotional connection, there certainly were days when miscommunication happened. I may have read something in one tone, while he took it to mean something completely different. We may have had a discussion and, without having the luxury of seeing when the other person actually stopped speaking, someone would start to talk while the other was still making their point, leaving one of us feeling the other was just interrupting or not listening. Most of the time we did a really good job given the circumstances, but there were those days that were absolutely more difficult.

By April I knew I was not going to last too much longer without having a discussion as to where this was going. We had not had that talk yet. And while I knew what I wanted, I had not yet actually shared the depth of my feelings with him (nor he with me). The unknown was terrifying but so was the thought of finding out the truth. What if he didn't feel the same? Would this all come crashing down? Would I lose him? Up until that point, I had been operating under the notion that keeping my feelings to myself would give me protection.

Fifty-eighth dating lesson learned: Once you have fallen, once you love, there is no protection. Your heart is open and there is no going back, whether you voice it or not.

Mr. Chicago had planned to come to New York in mid-April and then I was set to go to Chicago four days after to spend five days there. I made a conscious decision that after this amount of time we were about to spend together, that I would have no choice but to say something. I could not go on "in hiding" too much longer as I felt like I was going to explode with an "I love you" at any given moment.

The second night after he arrived in New York, we had an amazing evening. We went to Marissa and David's for dinner, followed by a fun night out with a few of my other friends. When it was time to end the evening, we hailed a cab and that is when the unexpected happened. After we told the cabbie where we were headed, he turned to look at me and said, "I need to know what you want. I need to know where you stand."

Granted, this bold statement came after a night of many shots he had with the bartender. Highly intoxicated was an understatement, but wasn't it known that high doses of alcohol were what let one's inhibitions down? Bring alcohol in to the mix and the truth would eventually be set free.

"Wow!" was the first thing I thought. I had once again assumed wrong in that I would have been the one who was going to have to bring this all up in another week. I had prepared myself to hear that he just could not commit, the distance was too much, he wasn't sure, and there were other girls…

How wrong I was! Apparently he had been feeling the same way I had since day one and had no idea where I stood. Could this really be happening? Had I somehow found myself lucky enough to be on the exact same page as someone else at the exact same time? Was I actually going to end up in a happy relationship? It was difficult to believe because I had gotten to a point where I was not sure this day was ever going to come. It all felt very surreal, as up until that point, there had been a part of me that was no longer sure if I was capable of loving to the level that I was now. But I had changed. Something in me had cracked open; something that had not been opened since the year 2000 — and even then, I did not feel THIS strongly.

We stayed up for a while that night talking things out. He said he had given me "just enough rope to hang myself with," followed by telling me "you never share how you feel about me, so I didn't know." And he was right. Here I thought I was so obvious, but in the end I had no idea he was clueless about how I felt. It was in that moment that I realized in order for this to work, I was going to have to just dive straight in, no holding back. So I did.

When I went to Chicago the following week he introduced me to his parents. Nothing like full steam ahead! But I was truly honored he wanted me to meet them, and while this was a pretty big deal to me, I made sure to maintain my composure. I went with it and we had a really nice time. Everything was seemingly falling in to place and I sometimes had to pinch myself; I could not believe after the past eight years of dating nonsense I was finally getting everything I wanted. Of course the one looming downside (as there had to be one) was the distance…

Until there was a second...

Mr. Chicago had come back east in early May for work and we spent a great night together. He flew in to Newark and I went to meet him there. We rented a car to drive what was supposed to be ten minutes to the hotel he was staying at. Unfortunately, he typed in the wrong address to his GPS — and forty minutes later we realized we were driving to Chicago! We broke in to hysterics at the stupidity of it all and that was how I knew I loved him as much as I did. It was raining, it was late, and we were both tired and hungry, but it did not matter. We were together. I could have easily gotten cranky and annoyed, but instead remained calm and enjoyed every second I spent with him. Eventually, we found our way to the hotel and enjoyed a great night of room service — and then other things I won't share the details of. It was truly a wonderful evening.

The next morning, I was off for work and he had to head down to Philadelphia for meetings. I remember I kissed him gently goodbye and said "I'll see you soon baby." He said "I love you," and I was off.

One week later he got a 30-day notice at work.

For the next few weeks I did all I could to put him in contact with everyone and anyone I knew who may have had a job opportunity or could lead him to one. I think I spent more of my day networking on his behalf than doing my own job. I was scared. I knew what losing a job could mean to a man and it was apparent that he was really starting to struggle with it. Not to mention there was the fact we could never forget - the long distance. Being unemployed was not exactly conducive to buying plane tickets every month.

I was so exasperated and frustrated with the whole situation. Why did this have to be happening to him? To us? Things had just gotten so good. Pulling the rug out on us this soon in our relationship was going to be hard to overcome. He was slipping a bit… he was feeling horrible on certain days and no matter what I said or did, I could not fix it or make him feel better. And the fact that I was trying to do so from a distance made it even harder. You can't just come home and hug the person, lay on the couch with them without saying a word — just BE there for them. Instead we had the phone, the stupid phone, where conversations were not always easy. I tried hard to be supportive, wanting him to know I was there for him, no matter what. And I really meant it. No matter what, I was not going anywhere — he had me for support and to lean on — the good and the bad. My heart was wide open to him — I was his for the taking.

Of course in the middle of all of this, I was still attempting to go along with "business as usual" and plan ahead for us. The job loss could have been a good or bad thing —he could have more time on his hands, he could come to New York more and stay longer while he job searched, maybe he would even move? If it meant for a little while we lived in New York until the economy fixed itself, then so be it. He would ask if he could show up on my doorstep if he needed, and I told him over and over that of course he could! But was that really what he wanted?

I would soon find out…

"The Unfortunate Departure Of Mr. Chicago"

I asked *Mr. Chicago* if he would plan to come to New York one particular weekend because my uncle's girlfriend was throwing him a surprise 50th birthday and a lot of my friends would be around that weekend as well. I thought it would be a great opportunity to not only get to spend some more time with him, but also help take his mind off the struggles he was dealing with from his unsuccessful job search. Plus I so badly wanted him to meet even more of the people that were important to me — not because I wanted to pressure him, but because I wanted him to feel included and be a part of the life I was living in NY. It was all out of the love I had for him and the love I wanted him to understand would always be there.

In full disclosure, I am a planner — one of my great attributes to some and one of my biggest vices to others — whereas he really did not scope things out the same way. We both knew this and I did not hide that aspect of myself. All I could ask was the understanding that it was okay for me to be me, and to just be honest if he could not do what I was asking. I thought that seemed pretty reasonable. And usually he agreed that it was, until now.

Based on all of the stress he was feeling from the loss of his job and financial stability, he seemed to have also lost his ability to be patient and accept my "planner-like" requests. I wanted to know he was coming this one particular weekend well in advance and he could not make that commitment in the moment I wanted him to. This led to a huge blow up argument that turned in to a week of silence so he could "think things over". Never a good sign when a man CHOOSES to think.

One week later we had a very upsetting phone call. He explained to me that while he loved me very deeply, he could not continue this long-distance relationship given the fact that he was unemployed. It was just not going to work. My head was spinning and all I wanted to do was convince him otherwise. I needed to tell him how much I cared, how much I understood — that I wanted to be there to support him and help him through this rough patch because that is what loving couples do.

What came out of my mouth instead?

"But what about me?"

Yes, after all of those thoughts running through my head, THOSE were the words I chose. I then followed up with what many girls make the grand mistake of doing — I pleaded to stay in touch and remain friends.

Fifty-ninth dating lesson learned: If you ever have the urge to "stay in touch" and "lessen the blow of the break up," fight it with every inch of your being. Nothing good will come of it.

He did not have the guts or heart to decline my request, so he did what a lot of men make the grand mistake of doing — he agreed to my plea, but all the while knew full well transitioning to long distance friends was not realistic. And then he played that role of "Houdini" that so many men had learned to play so well – disappearing into what felt like thin air.

In hindsight I am able to admit it was the best thing, but at the time I could not comprehend how or why he made the choice that he did. It was devastating. As a result of the pain and confusion I was feeling, I did the most embarrassing thing I have ever done to date in my dating career. I would hear stories of girls doing "crazy" things, yet that was never ever me. I always approached things with a rational mind. But you know, when you are really heartbroken, it is amazing what you may find yourself doing...

Interlude

"Miss Blogger"

Mr. Chicago's *best friend at the time had a blog. I knew about the blog and I also knew that* Mr. Chicago *had booked a trip (months prior) to go see this best friend of his in Hawaii. While I had no idea of his whereabouts in those first few weeks post break up, I knew exactly when he would be in Hawaii.*

When that day arrived, I checked the blog to see if there would be pictures of Mr. Chicago. *I did this for two reasons: First, I missed him. I was having a really hard time with managing those feelings. Second, I had convinced myself (when it came to break-ups, we often derive all sorts of crazy possibilities of what could be going on.) that* Mr. Chicago *had gotten back together with his ex and that there was this huge possibility she was now going to Hawaii with him. I took on my first stint as an FBI Agent to try to "uncover the truth".*

Sure enough, the day he arrived in Hawaii, there was a picture of him posted alone on a mountain, clearly on a hike. But was he really alone? Did his bff take the picture or were there others with him? Or worse, was he on a romantic hike with the ex I had convinced myself had accompanied him there?

And that was all it took; I started to check the blog incessantly to see if there would be more pictures. Could I "crack the code" on what was really going on? Was his ex-girlfriend really with him? Did he look sad? Was he having fun? I had become a relationship sleuth, trying to piece together what was going on with him halfway across the world.

Since I was working on a piece of business that summer that was quite slow, it allowed me to check an email at work, maybe call a client, and then check the blog. This became routine for a few days and something I had grown all too comfortable with. The more days that passed and I only saw pictures of the two guys posted, the better I felt.

Until the day I received an email...from Mr. Chicago.

While my heart initially skipped a beat seeing his name, when I read the subject line "Dave's Blog", my stomach immediately dropped. I opened the email to find the following, "I'm not quite sure what you're looking for, but I just thought you should know we can see every time you go on the blog." If I had had more food in my stomach that morning, I may have actually puked right then and there. Thank God for the break up diet.

Here I thought I was "mourning" in private, when in fact they could see every single time I looked at it?! I could not *even tell you how many times my IP address must have shown up; the thought of it made me cringe. The jig was up, and I had no place to hide. I was a total stalker; and totally caught. I wanted to die — or at the very least disappear into a very deep hole for a period of days, possibly weeks. Who knew that they could track IP addresses so that bloggers knew exactly who was checking their blogs at all times?*

Sixtieth dating lesson learned: Do not go and stalk other people's blogs — especially when those blogs have something to do with an ex. You will be discovered one way or another. And it will not be good.

Never in my life had I done anything like this — I had friends who would tell me insane stalker things they would do and I never could comprehend how they could act that way. But now it became apparent. In my case, I just simply missed him and had gotten myself in to a ridiculous and addictive FBI Agent routine. Once I got my composure back from the shock of it all, I sent a mass email to all of my girlfriends alerting them to the fact that they should NOT be going on blogs without understanding that the people whose blogs they are CAN see who was signing in to view them. In other words, DO NOT STALK A GUY WHO YOU MAY HAVE STARTED TO DATE OR AN EX BOYFRIEND! A few of my friends actually wrote back completely freaked out that they had been going on to blogs of the most recent guys they had started to date and they could not believe the people would be able to know due to the IP addresses.

A few years later I was at a birthday dinner for my friend Erica. Somehow at the dinner my friend Nikki got on the topic of all of the crazy things she had done while dating. My jaw was nearly scraping the floor as she divulged her insanity to the rest of us. At one point I interjected with "I swear, I did one thing once, got caught and was so mortified. I can NOT BELIEVE you did all of the things you just told us!" Of course the girls then probed me to re-tell my blog story. As I went through it, Erica's friend from D.C. who was visiting chimed in, "I have heard this story!" This was the first time I had ever met this girl, so there was no way she could have heard this story, right???

WRONG!

When I probed her, it turned out she was friends with a girl named Jenny. Jenny was my friend Sam's friend from college. My friends had warned all of their friends about blog stalking because of what happened to me. Yup. It was official—My story had gone National. I swear, only me!

I will say the aftermath of doing what I had done (and more so, getting caught) was horrendous. I was mortified and it felt like it was worst thing ever. Eventually I would be able to laugh about it, but had you told me then that I would ever be able to do anything but cry, I would have told you that you were crazy. It was amazing what time and distance from a situation will do...and what seems like the biggest deal in the world in the moment just becomes a funny story to tell later on.

Bottom line, I thought Mr. Chicago *was supposed to be Mr. Right, and I was supposed to be able to end this crazy dating streak.* Clearly that was not what happened and once again proved that with life, especially the part that requires you to engage with others in pursuit of your own personal fulfillment, anything was possible.

Interlude

"Miss Broken Hearted"

True heartbreak cracks you open. At least it did for me. After Mr. Chicago *and I broke up, I literally felt like my life had bottomed out. But the experience did truly force me to take a look inside myself and find the areas I needed to work on, areas that had become my Achilles heel or my demons, if you will. While the summer of 2009 was by far one of my hardest, it was also to date one of the biggest growing periods in my life. There was zero doubt that had* Mr. Chicago *and I had not broken up, I would absolutely not have evolved at all. Though the split was most certainly painful, it was also the most beneficial break up. I learned so many invaluable lessons:*

1. You have to put in the time to heal — there is just no fighting it.
2. Sometimes you do the unthinkable when you are heartbroken; something — or multiple things — that you normally would deem "crazy" otherwise. Embrace those situations for what they are, and realize they are just a

temporary reaction to a temporary situation. Frankly, you're allowed. Like Billy Joel says, you're only human — you're allowed to make your share of mistakes.

3. No matter what other people say, you have to believe what is right for you IS right. Go through your own healing in your own way.

4. You may think you can protect against heartbreak. But you can't.

5. It really is true that it's better to have loved and lost rather than to have never loved at all.

6. Being hard on yourself and blaming yourself is the natural tendency when a relationship doesn't work out the way you wanted it to. But no matter what you may have said or done, it wasn't going to change the outcome. If a person chooses to walk, they choose to walk.

7. While healing from heartbreak, learn to be kinder to yourself. You wouldn't be mean to your friend and you wouldn't be friends with someone who was mean to you. (According to Marissa, in the initial stages of this time in my life, I had "become harder on myself than I would be on Hitler". A fact that was true, and yet not okay!)

8. Your entire life's happiness <u>cannot</u> be wrapped up in whether or not you are in a relationship. You have to find happiness with yourself, within yourself, whether or not you have that "person" in your life.

9. Anger is very paralyzing. There is no sense in holding on to it for too long. If you are lucky

enough to have loved someone unconditionally — no matter what happens — find the forgiveness inside yourself and let it come out. Life is too short not to.

10. You cannot compare yourself to where your friends are, nor should you ever try. Just because some are married with babies does not mean you are a failure or are not "okay." Everyone has their own path to go down and sometimes those that are closest to you are on a path that is far different from the one you are walking down. And there is absolutely nothing wrong with that.

11. It could take a few years and a few more tries to get to the "why" — to that "hindsight is 20/20" — but eventually you will get there.

The truth was, dealing with the aftermath of my break up was something I thought I would just ignore. I figured I would just move right into the next step of my life, and that would be that. It was so painful that I was petrified of actually having to feel it. But I quickly learned that approach was not going to work for me and there was not much I could do about it. I had to deal and I had to let myself sit in it if I was ever going to heal. So with the help of therapy, amazing friends and family, some spiritual guides, and a LOT of massage, reiki, reflexology and facials I spent a lot of hard-earned money on in the Metropolitan area, I got through it and began my journey to moving on.

However, I could not believe I had to get back in to the crazy dating world again. BUT I had to. I was not going to give up on finding true love, so back in to the pool I dove and the swim certainly proved to be interesting.

Frog #26

"Mr. WAY Too Much Too Fast"

About 2 months after this now infamous break up, my best friend from college, Jodi, called and said she had a great guy to set me up with. She had just met him the weekend before at a friend's house in Philly. Of course she was bombed after drinking many glasses of wine, but swore she had good radar on this.

Jodi said he was very inquisitive and asked a million questions about me. She liked this and she liked him. Looking back at that period in time, I was probably not quite ready to be dating again. But I had worked through some of it and wanted the final pain to go away, so I figured what the hell, if this guy was right for me then I did not want to pass up the opportunity. No matter what, I was not going to be completely defeated by my heartbreak! I told her to give him my number and just like that, my digits were his.

Sixty-first dating lesson learned: Those who do not learn from their past are doomed to repeat it… I had quickly forgotten how sacred my phone number was and paid the price.

Two nights later I received a call. We had a nice conversation and this guy seemed like a cool, interesting person (cool, interesting… I really needed to come up with better adjectives to describe someone on their first screening). I did not feel threatened and I enjoyed the conversation, so my thought was, "What more could I really expect at this point?"

There were downsides though, the first being that he lived in Philly. Unfortunately, this did not allow for either of us to pull the "Let's meet tomorrow night for a drink" routine. No, we had to plan in advance…two weeks in advance actually. That was the first time he would be able to make it up to the city. For me this was a bit of a bummer because I really did not want to invest much time in to this guy without ever having met him. At the sake of sounding too blunt, I just wanted to get the drink over with.

Yes, I know what you must be thinking. My current dating outlook was pretty meager. But hey, I was at least trying! I eventually accepted the long distance situation for what it was and figured we would make a plan the next time we spoke. And that would be that until the day came to meet, right?

Wrong.

Mr. WAY Too Much Too Fast proceeded to call me almost <u>every</u> day for the next few days. At first I thought he was nice and it was endearing that he was interested enough by my conversation to want to speak to me so much. I thought it was nice that he remembered every last word I said. I thought it was nice he would follow up a day later with even more thoughtful responses. I thought it was nice that he was that in tune with me. I thought it was nice until I didn't think it was nice.

Sixty-second dating lesson learned: Those who do not learn from the past are doomed to repeat it… I had quickly forgotten how sacred my phone number was and paid the price (yes I repeated this message to ensure this time it was etched in my brain forever).

After one of many phone calls, I hung up and realized I did not have a clue as to what this guy looked like. I needed to see pictures immediately before I really committed to meeting him, so I asked him over e-mail to send me some. He wrote me a few e-mails before the actual pictures were finally sent, explaining that he needed to get the pictures downloaded on to some disc. That probably should have been the first clue that something was awry…especially with us living in the world of Facebook, online dating and blogging. Surely this guy had some regular digital pictures saved on his computer, right? He had now created this additional anticipation of me having to wait for the pictures — compounded by the fact that Jodi had started to question if I was going to find him attractive. Johnny Come Lately had suddenly come to the realization that maybe her wine goggles were more fogged up than she initially thought the night she had met him.

Sixty-third dating lesson learned: Always question a friend's judgment when she is intoxicated. ALWAYS.

Oy vey, what I had gotten myself in to?!

When I finally received the e-mail with the pictures attached, I understood the delay and the need to transfer them on to a disc. I clicked on the first picture, and to my complete surprise, I was met with a picture of a little boy in a speedo bathing suit. There was literally a child staring back at me on my computer screen; a young boy who could not have been more than three years old. Was this a joke? Surely it had to be a mistake! But as I clicked on attachments two and three, much to my chagrin, pictures of — you guessed it — the same little boy! Was this supposed to be cute? If it was, I was not feeling it. Pictures four, five and six of him arrived a few minutes later as an adult, thank God. But by then I was turned off. Unless this guy was Patrick "McDreamy" Dempsey's long-lost twin, he just lost about 100 points with me. Starting at negative 100 with a girl whose heart was still recovering from being smashed in to pieces was not a good place to be. Granted it was not his fault I was where I was emotionally, but the cards were not in his favor.

For a split second, I had that moment of questioning myself. Was I being too critical? Was it normal for someone to send these types of pictures? Should I have found this cute? Was I wrong for thinking this was weird? After relaying the story to a few friends, I was reassured the answer to all of my questions was NO.

Sixty-fourth dating lesson learned: When a guy sends you pictures of himself at age three before you've even met, don't question your skepticism — it IS weird.

Over the next few days, *Mr. WAY Too Much Too Fast* proceeded to call me a few more times. He left long-winded voicemails with lots of details and lots of information; too much information. I was starting to go to the really bad place and by the weekend, I was completely turned off. It was one thing to showcase some persistence and interest. It was something very different when someone shows signs of desperation.

Sixty-fifth dating lesson learned: When a guy starts to care a seemingly inordinate amount before having ever met you, you need to question it.

The next time we spoke, he wanted to solidify our plans for the following weekend. He actually suggested spending the entire day and evening with me! Red flags immediately went up, and the voice in my head screamed "Hell no!"

I know I had spent an entire weekend with *Mr. Chicago* the first time we met, but I also knew he was the exception to the rule. I was not committing to an entire day and evening with a guy whose first visual impression of himself was as a three-year-old in a banana hammock. There was a huge possibility (and the more I spoke to him, the more I knew how huge it was) that I was going to make it through one drink and want to bolt. There was no other option for me but to decline his full day offer, suggest we just meet in the evening, and then hope we could end all further communication until this looming date arrived. Luck was not on my side with this one and my hopes were sadly crushed when he called two more times over the next day and a half.

I waited each time to call him back. In fact, I did not even return his second call until Monday night. I dialed, and the phone began to ring.

Ring. Ring. Was it going to go to voicemail? Could I be this lucky? Ring. Ring…

Yes! I actually got his voicemail and I was psyched! I left my short message but the fact I was this happy probably was not a good sign,

"Looks like I missed you. Hope you are out doing something fun. No need to call me back. We can catch up when we meet up on Saturday. Bye."

I hung up the phone feeling like I had FINALLY nipped the communication in the bud.

I was not that lucky. Within three minutes, I received a call back — I kid you not. I did not answer. And while this may seem somewhat mean-spirited, I frankly was not in the mood and I thought I had made it clear there was no reason to call me back. I spelled it out, did I not? Two minutes later, I received a text. When I read the text and listened to the voicemail, both went on and on about why he didn't answer my call. He was basically apologizing as if he owed me an explanation. He was on the phone with his friend in India and he felt like he couldn't interrupt to take the call waiting. Well no shit Captain Obvious! If he HAD done that, I would have hung up right then and there.

Some might be questioning my harshness and say "So what? This guy was actually nice, so what the hell is wrong with YOU Courtney?"

And I could not disagree that this guy was nothing short of nice, but at the same time I was just trying to get my feet wet with dating again — likely too soon — and this guy was acting like my boyfriend before we even met. I felt pushed up against a wall. And I could not breathe. I wanted out. It was way too much, way too fast.

After speaking to Jodi, as well as my therapist, we all agreed my assessment of the situation was spot on. I was going to have to bail. I could not go out with him. I was dreading it and that was not a good feeling to have.

Sixty-sixth dating lesson learned: Forcing yourself because you feel bad or because you think you are "supposed to" do something when it comes to relationships — or ANYTHING for that matter — is NO good.

The next day, I elected to let him know it wasn't going to happen as far as us getting together. I sent him an email, which I thought would be best.

Dear Mr. WAY Too Much Too Fast,

Hope you are doing well...
I actually wanted to write because I have to be honest about something...I did just recently break up with someone, but it was a pretty intense situation. Anyway, I thought I was ready to jump in to dating again but in the last week I'm realizing I'm not quite there yet. Part of me wants to push through and have you come up here and meet you, but I have to do what feels right for me and I wanted to be honest about that. I'd hate for you to come all the way up here and I'm just not in the right frame of mind, and then you've made the trip up from Philly :) I'm just sort of thinking it may be better if when I make it down to visit Jodi in the next month or so at some point, maybe we can all meet up for a drink and I can meet you then — a situation with a little less pressure, as its just where I'm at for the moment.
I'm sorry to have started to go down this path and now put the stop on it but I really thought I was more ready than I am. You seem like a really nice, great guy, so I want to just be honest with you and really myself as well in this.
I hope you understand. I really believe honesty is the best policy and at the end the day, the place I'm in right now, I have to just do what is right for me.
Well I hope you have a good night and again, that you understand.

To which I received this response….

Hey Court,

I hope we get a chance to meet-up when you are in Philly. No problem on the Saturday plan. Although I had hoped we could meet, get a drink, wander off into an unpredictable evening of exquisite dining, insightful conversation, salsa dancing and watching the sun rise together, I can understand how that might be too much too soon. Thanks for being communicative about your feelings. I wouldn't want the time together to be anything other than fun. If I put the rush on you, then I can slow the roll. I tried to keep it loose. If anything, let's catch-up sometime again to chat and if you feel comfortable talking, we can stick to that. You are cool with me. I'll be in NYC on Saturday and hope you have a good weekend wherever you are.

I knew I had made the right decision. And even though this guy was a "nice" guy and maybe some of you think I missed the boat on my future husband, I knew in my gut it was not right.

In addition to all of the above, I found out after the fact that he lived at home with his parents. Granted it was outstanding circumstances that led to this, but still, how was I even going to have a long-distance relationship with someone who lived at home? The answer was simple — I wasn't.

Frog #27

"Mr. Should"

Mr. Should was the guy I "should" date. He was the guy I "should" like. He was the guy I "should" end up in a relationship with. This latest *Mr. Should* was not the first *Mr. Should* guy I had ever dated but he would be the last.

Sixty-seventh dating lesson learned: The English language really needs to do away with the word "should."

I was introduced to the third *Mr. Should* through Marissa and our mutual friend Mike. They were out in the Hamptons one weekend during the summer of 2009 when they met this guy and together decided he & I would be a great match. When Marissa called to "sell" me on him, the conversation went something like this, "Hi, I met this great guy and I really think he would be someone you will like. But there are four negatives."

And I was supposed to show nothing less than sheer enthusiasm and excitement?!

Lucky for her, of the four she listed, only one actually bothered me — his age. He was a little older than I wanted to go for, but he apparently didn't look or act it, so after an internal deliberation, I told myself to get past it. The other three were things that I, unlike Marissa, could look past: He was a social smoker (not great but not a deal breaker for me), he had called off his engagement six months prior (if he was ready to date, so was I), and he lived in the west village and I was on the Upper East Side. To some, this would be a long distance relationship. Considering I traveled 700 miles by plane in my last relationship, I could handle the four-mile cab ride.

Based on our busy schedules, *Mr. Should* and I were finally able to get together after Labor Day. I was looking forward to meeting him, and he definitely sounded cool and nice (there I go again using those very descriptive adjectives. But hey, at least it wasn't others like crazy and weird). We met on a Sunday night (nothing like drinking on a Sunday night) and had a good time. He was cute and personable, the conversation flowed and I enjoyed myself. He paid for drinks, he walked me home and he even texted to say he had a great time. He did ALL of the right things. I was encouraged by the course of the events, so we made plans to go out again the following Wednesday.

In the meantime he asked for my email, so we began to exchange messages all day long. I was happy because I believed once I had established I didn't want to run for hills from a guy, this was another way to get to know someone better. The more opportunities I had to interact directly with someone, the easier it was to keep the momentum going until the next time we would see each other. It usually allowed for a deeper connection to begin and I loved how elated I would feel when I had a new message from my latest love interest.

After a few days of emailing with *Mr. Should*, I started to realize a few things. First, he did not make me laugh — at all. Second, our conversations were very basic. I could tell you everything he was doing throughout his day but I could not tell you a thing about him, who he was or what he was about. Third, as a result of one and two, I was no longer excited when his name popped up in my inbox. I wasn't annoyed, but I wasn't excited. It felt no different than receiving an email from a friend. And while I loved my friends, when I saw "Marissa" pop up in my mail, my heart certainly didn't skip that beat from excitement. And it didn't for *Mr. Should* either.

All in all, these were not great signs. And believe me when I say I wanted so badly to feel "it". This guy was sweet, kind, adorable, successful, family-oriented, and loved to travel; if someone were to have asked me what I was looking for in the opposite sex, he fit the description perfectly. It was because of this I felt I had no choice but to give it my "third-date rule." As I eluded to much earlier in my dating career, I had made a conscious decision to give these types of situations at least three times to see if the "it" factor was delayed or if was just never going to show up.

I came down with a cold just in time for date two but I knew no matter what I had to see this guy again, so I forced myself to go anyway. I wanted to feel something — even just a little flutter, some intrigue, SOMETHING that gave me a sign that I should continue to date him. And the only way for that to happen was for me to go out with him that night, cold or no cold.

While the ambiance, food, drinks and company were all decent that night I could not get a sense for who this guy was. I didn't feel as though we were truly connecting. When I attempted to pry a little about his idiosyncrasies — those things that made him unique — he would divert the conversation elsewhere. And what bothered me even more was the fact he was clearly not interested to know mine. It all started to feel very superficial, almost cosmetic. I can have basic conversation all day long with just about anyone, but if I was going to consider dating you and if you wanted me to have feelings for you, there was going to have to be something more than just "my dog wouldn't poop this morning so I was late to work" and "my mom is coming to visit next weekend". If I can't get passed general facts, getting beyond just a friendship was likely not going to be possible. While this was only date two, we had been talking over text or email for weeks now and frankly other than being a good kisser, there was nothing about the way we seemed to be connecting (or not connecting) that was drawing me to want get closer to him.

In truth, I felt nothing. I was numb. I started to think maybe it was a result of not being completely over *Mr. Chicago* yet. I didn't want this to be the reason so I pushed the thought away and tried to remain present throughout the rest of the date.

After he paid the bill, he offered to take me to Duane Reade to buy some medicine for my cold. We were half way down the flu isle, when he pulled me towards him and kissed me. Normally I would think this was a hot move; indicating he had zero regard for his own health and was more concerned with establishing the interest he had in me. But bold and all, I felt nothing.

I could have been kissing the wall with how little I felt and that was NOT a good feeling. By now I "should" have been feeling something. I went home that night and I was empty. Not good. This meant crying for the next hour over *Mr. Chicago*, longing for the feeling I had when I first kissed him. That sensation was what I wanted to feel. That was what I was supposed to feel, not nothing.

Despite my state of mind post-date two, and against my better judgment, I chose not to end things with *Mr. Should*. While it would reveal itself soon enough, my inner confidence to not care about being called "too selective and finicky" had not yet been discovered; I gave in to the need to want to please my persistent friends who so desperately wanted to see me with someone. And so I ended up going out with *Mr. Should* one or two more times. I actually could not even recall the exact number, which tells you how little impact the time I had spent with him had on me. But when he asked me out the fifth or sixth (?) time, I knew I could not go just because I thought I "should." I had FINALLY grasped the notion it was time to live my life for me and not to please everyone else.

Sixty-eighth dating lesson learned: When you feel numb kissing someone, you're simply "Just Not That In to Them."(Just as the infamous book and subsequent movie suggest)

First, I wrote him a very nice email to explain how I was feeling. Second, I broke the news to Marissa. While I felt completely relieved, I was not sure who took the news harder — *Mr. Should* or my defeated best friend.

Sixty-ninth first dating lesson learned: You cannot date someone just because your best friend wants you to find the love of your life quite possibly as much, or even more, than you do.

I had learned to live with disappointment, and she would too.

Interlude

"Miss Pause and Reflect"

After this last Frog I walked away from, I realized I needed to put a big pause on my dating career. I needed to stop, focus and ask myself not only what I wanted out of a relationship, but also what I wanted out of life. I needed to start to get really honest with myself. And what I discovered was, I was not happy. And it was not just about not having found my person yet; it was more than that and I needed to do some serious soul searching to figure out what it was that was going to make me happy.

Following many analytical discussions with friends, my therapist, my family, and sitting alone a lot and thinking, I realized I needed a major change to happen in my life. It had all become completely redundant — and quite frankly, boring. I needed a major shakeup and I needed to do something solely for myself. And that is when I finally came to the conclusion I needed to move.

After visiting Dom (as a reminder, he was my best friend from college who lived in Chicago) a number of times during the fall of 2009, I had fallen back in love. And as much as

I love Dom with all of my heart, it was not he who I was in love with (if you recall, he is gay). Instead, I was having a love affair with the city of Chicago and was faced with having to make the tough decision to pick up my life and move to a new city, away from everything and everyone I knew, and yes, to the city where Mr. Chicago resided. Despite what many likely thought, I was not moving there for him. I made sure to do a ton of soul searching, with my therapist I might add, to ensure that the move was the right one for me personally and that my motives were intact. As easy as it likely was for people to determine the impetus behind my move was him, there was NO WAY I would uproot my life – leave my family, friends, and amazing job – for a guy I had not spoken to in over six months and would likely never speak to again. I had dated guys that lived on the same block as I had in NY and I never saw them one time after things ended. Chicago is the 3rd largest DMA in the country – the likelihood of me even running in to Mr. Chicago was slim to none and I wanted it that way. Bumping into an ex unexpectedly was NEVER a fun time. My therapist saw the fear and shear horror I had on my face at the thought of a "Mr. Chicago run-in", all while still wanting to move to the Windy City, and she knew I was making the move for the right reasons.

I flew to the Midwest one more time in December 2009 to make my final decision. I did not stay with Dom, but instead bunked in a hotel in Lincoln Park on my own. After all, this was what it would be like when I moved, right? I would be on my own and could not rely solely on Dom for everything. I would have to make new friends and find my own way around.

Once I proved to myself on that last trip that I could do this, and after a lengthy conversation with my wise friend Nicole who had made a similar decision for herself a few years prior (picking up and moving to NY from the Midwest) said "Worse than going is not going. If you choose the latter, you will never know. If you go and hate it, you can always move back" (the best advice I had heard in a long time), I made my official decision - I was moving to Chicago!

In March 2010 I hopped on a plane for the night, interviewed for a job and signed a lease that would start April 15, 2010. I felt excited and invigorated in a way I had not in a VERY long time! I was ready for the change and knew I needed it. However, this kind of a decision (even once it had been made) did not come without a ton of anxiety — leaving my comfort zone, leaving my family and friends, leaving a city behind that I had lived in for 11 years. Luckily I had discovered a phrase that I had come to love and it was what gave me the strength to do what I knew I needed to do during the days I felt uneasy: "Change of any sort takes courage." I printed the saying and put it in a frame so that I could see it every day and read it over and over and over again. It helped remind me why I was embarking down this new road in the journey of my life; I lived by those words, and if nothing else, I was so proud of myself for making a decision to change my life — even if this drastic change WAS scary at times.

About four months after my big move, I had settled in and gotten acclimated to my new home. I was having fun, going out and taking in all my new city on the shores of Lake

Michigan had to offer. I loved my friends, I loved my apartment, I loved my job — frankly, I loved Chicago. I finally felt alive again and I was enjoying it. I did not want anything to bring me down or interrupt the bliss that I had discovered; therefore I made a point to dismiss any men from my life. For the first months I was there, I really did not want to mess with how great I felt. It got to the point where my friend Mike back in New York expressed serious concern that I had taken a secret life long oath of celibacy. He would later refer to this period of time as "The Year of the Nun".

But at the end of the day, I knew I still wanted to find the love of my life, and the only way to do that was to expose myself to the opposite sex. So eventually I took a deep breath, hoped for the best, and re-opened that door, allowing myself the opportunity to meet men in the Windy City.

So with that, I give you my dating experiences in Chitown.

Frog #28

"Mr. Cobweb Cleaner"

It was the end of June 2010 and a friend of mine was having a birthday party at a bar we had been hanging out at quite frequently and I was excited for another fun night out in Chicago; it seemed every time I went out, I had a blast. The summer had come early, it was absolutely beautiful out, and I was truly feeling great! Back in New York, I had begun to anticipate who I may meet every time I went out. Would there be cute guys there? Would I have an instant connection with someone? Would "Mr. Right" be there? There were times I would force myself to go out just because of the "What If" factor – "What if I missed the opportunity to meet him?", "What if he was there and I didn't go?" But in Chicago, I found that my mentality had changed. I didn't think like this. Instead, I was so happy to feel good and be experiencing all of this "newness" in my life, and that was enough. So as I headed out for my friend's party that night, I was just simply looking forward to hanging out and having a great time.

Seventieth dating lesson learned: Your mindset and energy really do play a role in how you attract the opposite sex.

Feeling almost like I did back at 22 when I first graduated college, the last thing I was looking for that particular night was to meet a guy. But of course as I sat on a stool, smiling and sipping my vodka club with a lime, a group of three guys approached me. It was like moths to a flame. I did nothing to encourage this except that I was simply in a great place and clearly exuded positive, light-hearted energy. They could not get enough of me, asking a million questions about my move, where I grew up, why Chicago, what I did for a living. Eventually the three dwindled to two, and then two dropped down to just one. And it was quite clear he and I had chemistry. He was cute, funny, sarcastic, and yet he seemed to have a real sensitive side, as he opened up to me about his job loss that had led to his divorce and the devastation of it all. And just like that, I was completely intrigued once again by someone of the opposite sex.

Seventy-first dating lesson learned: Whether you want it or not, when there's chemistry, there's chemistry. There's no denying or fighting it, so you might as well just surrender to it.

After a few more drinks, I found myself with this guy at the pizza place down the street eating what he claimed to be the pie "most similar to New York pizza." That fact was debatable, but for some reason I did not want to disappoint the guy, so I just smiled and said "Oh yeah, it's great. I feel right at home!" From there, we headed to my apartment, making our way to the 7th-floor rooftop where there were pretty lights and fire pits. After about ten seconds in this romantic scenery, I was making out again with someone of the opposite sex. Things progressed, he ended up staying over that night, and with that, *Mr. Cobweb Cleaner* was born — the man who took my year-long self-imposed "nun hood," as Mike continued to call it, and brought me back to the world of practicing safe sex.

The next morning, he INSISTED on taking me for breakfast to what he claimed to be "the place that has bagels that are most similar to those in New York." I began to sense a theme that he either wanted to prove to me that Chicago was just as great as New York (despite the fact I already thought it was better) or he just wanted to make me feel at home. Either way, I was going with it.

While the bagels were nowhere near the greatness of a New York City bagel, the time I was having with him was fantastic. We talked a lot about life — where we had been, some of the hardships we each had gone through — while we drove around and listened to country music (his favorite music genre). When he dropped me off at

my apartment a few hours later, he said he wanted to see me soon…
and just like that, I was once again dating.

Now had I been more in tune to the things he told me during our first
night together, I would have realized that we were absolutely not
meant for each other. We were so completely different. But, as
things sometimes go, we do not always see those things because we
are just having fun. I liked this guy and it had been so long since I
had felt a physical connection to a guy that I ignored the obvious.
Instead I convinced myself that just because he was a devout
Catholic and churchgoer, it didn't matter. If it came down to it, we
would work that part out. Besides, I was just getting my feet back in
to the dating waters and believed I didn't need to pay attention to the
obvious right now… right?!

*Seventy-second dating lesson learned: Being honest with yourself is
not always easy, but the consequences of NOT being honest with
yourself are often even harder*

So as I continued to convince myself I was "just having fun," *Mr.
Cobweb Cleaner* and I would text back and forth all day long, he
would call me at night, we would banter — and to what should have
come as no shock at all, I started to actually like him. It felt good on
the surface to like someone again. To be excited to hear from
someone again. But unfortunately, the surface feelings were
drowning out the deeper gut feelings that said "He's not for you!
Walk away before he does!"

It was too bad those little voices could not have shouted louder
because after just a few short weeks in to this tryst, *Mr. Cobweb
Cleaner* went radio silent. Given the fact we had friends in common
and would see each other again, I was actually shocked he could do a
full 180° almost overnight.

*Seventy-third dating lesson learned: Never under-estimate the
actions of a cowardly man*

The truth was that if men would stop pulling the Houdini act and just
be straight right away there would be a lot less confusion when it

came to dating. What men did not realize was most women became irrational as a result of their senseless actions. Women will spend days wondering what happened, what they did, and why all of a sudden this guy hates them, when really it typically just boiled down to one simple fact — he simply did not think she was "the one." But rather than have a somewhat difficult conversation, a guy will pull away, stop making the effort he once had, or altogether disappear so that any girl with half a brain would know right away something was wrong. I had seen this happen over and over and over with many of my friends, as well as with myself. And I was over it. I was sick of men being complete cowards and not having the decency to have a conversation just because it may make them feel slightly uncomfortable. Weren't men supposed to have balls?

I decided I was not going to be the "wounded bird" or "crazy girl" who sat around left to wonder and feel horrible. Nope. That was not going to work for me. I had no choice but be the "bigger man" and call him out. Of course when I did, he apologized profusely and said he wasn't sure what to say, "There's no excuse for my actions. The bottom line was I just did not see us together long term."

The truth of the matter was he was right! We definitely were not meant for each other in the long run. I had felt and known the same but had just chosen to ignore it for the thrill of having a man back in my life. Had we continued to date for a bit longer, I may have even been the one to end things. So why it was so hard for him to have had a conversation with me about how he was feeling right off the bat versus going radio silent was beyond me.

Seventy-fourth dating lesson learned: To Mr. Cobweb Cleaner *and All the Other Mr.'s Out There like You — you are not that amazing*

Women will not die just because a man does not want to date us any longer. So please guys, get over yourselves, grow some balls and just be straight with the women you are dating. It will likely result in a lot less unnecessary anger, hurt, and confusion. This was my wish. Would it ever become the standard in dating? My gut told me no, but I would continue to at least remain prudently optimistic.

On a positive note, my days of being a "nun" were officially over. There was no going back. I had reignited a good feeling by connecting with a man. And regardless of the fact that *Mr. Cobweb Cleaner* was not going to be in my life long term, I knew I wanted and needed to feel again. So with that, it was another frog down and my quest to find Mr. Right continued.

Frog #'s 28 & 29

"Mr. Heebie-Jeebies & Mr. McShady"

Part One – Mr. Heebie-Jeebies

I decided it was time for me to re-enter the world of online dating, Chicago style, so I rejoined Match.com in August of 2010. I had broken my no-hook-up streak with *Mr. Cob Web Cleaner* and it was time to push that cracked door wide open and start to explore the male population in my new city.

The funny thing I had learned about online dating in New York City was that people were on the site for so long that most of the time they continued to see the same profiles over and over again. So if you had not been on in a while, or ever, the moment you signed up every guy within 100 miles of your house would email you. It was like testing the waters of the big ocean -- you dip your foot in, but all of the sharks smell the blood and come barreling towards you, hoping to get a bite of your leg.

Seventy-fifth lesson learned: Online dating in Chicago matches that of New York. And there were a lot of sharks out there.

Within a day, I had half the single men between the ages of 32-40 emailing, winking at, and IM'ing me. It was an online dating version of Shark Week. But because of all of the lessons I had learned while dating in New York City, I knew I had to be more selective. I was not going to engage in conversation with just anybody, and they were going to have to pass a more laborious screening process before we went on a date.

After I eliminated about 98 percent of those that had reached out, I took a liking to this one guy who was a 32-year-old divorced dad from the suburbs of Chicago. He seemed funny, smart, kind-hearted, ambitious, and it was clear he was a great dad. So when he asked, I accepted his offer to meet him for a drink after work.

The only sad part was, I stopped getting excited for online blind dates. Even though it was a new city and new kind of men, I had been through too much and knew too much to allow myself that naive luxury. I obviously did not want to be this way. I WANTED to be excited. But to allow myself to feel that was no longer possible. So I learned to settle for "cautiously hopeful."

Seventy-sixth dating lesson learned: As you get older and wiser, you may find yourself sometimes longing for days where "What you don't know won't hurt you" were still possible.

As I approached my next date at the bar, he stood right up like a gentleman and pulled a chair out for me. He then handed me the menu so that I could order a drink and relax. Once our cocktails arrived, we got in to a great conversation where we realized we had both been through a lot in our lives. He seemed way more mature than 32 and I felt comfortable with him immediately. I just could not tell if it was in more of a friend way or if there was a romantic chemistry between us. I decided to table figuring that out on date one and allowed myself to enjoy a nice discussion with a new person.

We ended up staying out for a few hours before I started to get tired and stressed thinking about the work I had to get done the next day. As the gentleman that he had been all evening, he helped me put on my jacket, walked me outside and hailed me a cab. But before I got in, he pulled me towards him and kissed me. It was strange as I wasn't sure that I wanted him to kiss me; I had been unsure all night as to what I was feeling. I decided to chalk it up to the idea that maybe I had built my own Great Wall of China against first dates when they were either a result of meeting online or a blind set up. And that no matter what may have been between us, I was not going to allow myself to get swept up in it right away.

It seemed like a good enough theory to me, so I was sticking to it.

Seventy-seventh dating lesson learned: Convincing yourself of various theories as to why you may not feel something about a perfectly normal, sweet guy will not get you what you are looking for.

Before I was halfway home, he texted to let me know how great I was and that he wanted to see me the following weekend. I think I gave it a half smile, as who wouldn't be at least somewhat happy to read something sweet like that? But it did not ignite any feeling inside of me; it was nothing bad, yet it was not good either. I was typically clear about my feelings, but this one had me stumped.

I chalked it up to that Great Wall of China rationale and texted back, "Sure! That sounds great!" I felt as though I was on autopilot, using exclamation points for his sake, but knowing my enthusiasm was nothing short of fake.

By the time Saturday rolled around, this guy had texted me a few times. And while I responded every time, I had lost interest. There was something that did not feel right and with every text, I felt a shudder of annoyance run through my whole body. But I also felt guilty about the way I felt. Why did he give me such a weird feeling? Why was the Great Wall inside of me growing bigger and bigger instead of smaller and smaller? I could not come up with a solid answer, so I knew the only way to know for sure was to meet him and his friends out that night.

It did not take a lot of convincing to get my friends to accompany me. All I had to say was "He is bringing some cute, single friends," and they were sold. What was going to take a lot of convincing was for me to like this guy.

The second I walked in to the bar and saw him, my body tensed up. I was not excited. I did not feel that flutter you get in your stomach when you see a guy you like. In fact, it was the complete opposite. So when he came up and kissed me hello — on the mouth (ick), put his arms around me and kept them wrapped around my waist — I turned in to the tin man (or tin woman). I was stiff and completely uncomfortable. This guy had managed to give me the heebie-jeebies with the touch of his hand.

Seventy-eighth dating lesson learned: If you feel the heebie-jeebies, there's not a shadow of a doubt — You're Just Not That In To Him.

I had to get out of this situation, and I needed to do it quickly. But how was I going to extricate myself from his grasp?

Enter Part Two – Mr. McShady

I wiggled my body out of *Mr. Heebie-Jeebies* firm grasp by offering to get him a drink at the bar, where I saw one of his friends sipping his drink. As I made my way toward him, we made eye contact, and it was intense. I walked right up to him and engaged in conversation. He was way more my type physically — tall, lean, and brown hair with piercing blue eyes. He was hot. But at this point, I would have been happy to talk to anyone if it meant I no longer had to be within a foot of *Mr. Heebie-Jeebies*.

As I stood there waiting for the drinks I had ordered, *Mr. Heebie-Jeebies'* friend and I struck up a conversation. I was engaged. I was intrigued. I felt flutters.

Was this allowed? Was I violating some Match.com rule that said, "Thou shall not flirt with a Match guy's friend in front of him?" In true girl fashion, I grabbed two of my friends and dragged them to our bar conference room, aka the bathroom, and explained the situation.

Seventy-ninth dating lesson learned: I should have been going to my single friends, and my single friends only, for advice on dating. They just understood the territory much better than the marrieds.

Without any hesitation, my friends gave me the approval to move in on this new guy. How often did we find that random connection with someone? I had gone on just one date with *Mr. Heebie-Jeebies* and didn't really "owe" him anything. I didn't feel it. I wasn't pretending to. That was it, end of story. However, I did feel it with the guy I left standing at the bar. After a few more words of encouragement from my friends, I headed back to him to get my flirt on.

And boy did I! I had forgotten all about *Mr. Heebie-Jeebies* and the fact I had told him I was going to get him a drink (my reason for wiggling out of his tight grasp). I was completely in to his friend and was not hiding it at all. I did feel a slight twinge of guilt, but I ignored it. If I was out to meet my Mr. Right, and I already figured out that it wasn't him, why waste anyone's time?

After I gave my number to my new guy (of course on the sly), I decided to call it a night. *Mr. Heebie-Jeebies* was no fool. He knew it was over between us and that I was clearly in to another guy. He gave me a little bit of a hard time when I went to say good-bye, but I had to grin and take it. After all, this was by far the biggest blow off I had ever executed. I knew that if I were in his shoes, I would be writing a chapter called "Mr. Douche Bag" about his friend, and "Ms. Bitch" about me. But I wasn't in his shoes. I was in mine. So I did what was right for me.

The following Friday I had a date with my new hottie. I was psyched and was looking forward to seeing him again. He asked me to meet at this amazing pizza restaurant in Lincoln Park, and when the cab pulled up, he was already there. He stood leaning against the wall next to the entrance and waited for my cab to come to a stop. He looked so dapper in his long black coat and the Burberry scarf he had tied tightly around his neck. He walked over to my cab, helped me out, and The Great Wall of China was demolished within seconds; I felt anything but the heebie-jeebies and could not wait to kiss this guy!

Dinner was really fun and the after party at my place was even better. We drank some wine and made out like crazy. I kept it fairly PG-13 — I liked this guy and wanted to see where things could go. He stayed until close to 3 a.m. when we both decided we were exhausted and it was time to call it a night.

As we said our good-byes, he casually mentioned he would be traveling a lot the next week and would "be in touch." If you talk to any single girl, they will tell you they despise the "I'll be in touch" at the end of a good date. The unknown of the next steps in dating was excruciating. When you wanted to see someone again, but had to wait for him to ask, it was nothing short of awful. As soon as the "I'll be in touch" was muttered, you realized there was a huge possibility you may never see them again. It was never a good situation to be in, and yet there I sat — exactly where I did not want to be.

Had I described this uncertainty to my married friends, they would have told me I was nuts and overthinking everything. Lucky for me, I had finally smartened up and relied on my single friends to be my sounding board. They got it. They knew the feeling I had because they too had felt it many a time. I no longer felt alone and "crazy" (silver lining, right?).

With that, I checked my phone multiple times a day to see if he had texted or called, but I had that impending gut feeling telling me he was never going to. I even went as far as to shut off my cell one night to stop myself from looking every few minutes, holding out hope that when I turned it back on in the morning, I would have a missed call or text from him.

No such luck.

Eightieth dating lesson learned: There is something to be said about those old clichés like "What goes around comes around" and "Karma is a bitch."

Was this my payback for being shady myself the week before? How could a guy once again act so in to me one minute and then disappear, never to be heard from the next?

The answers to the aforementioned two questions were simple.

1) Yes, it was most certainly my payback.

2) He proved as recent as the weekend before just how shady he could be. Only this time I was the victim.

While I apologized to the Universe for my own hot minute of poor behavior, *Mr. McShady* was born.

Eighty-first dating lesson learned: Always remember the golden rule -do unto others as you want done to you

While I had no regrets for following my heart and walking away from *Mr. Heebie-Jeebies*, I definitely could have handled the situation with more grace and class. I hoped the Universe felt my remorse and did not have any further punishments in store for me.

By lesson eighty-one, I had started to grow quite tired of learning: I was ready for graduation.

Frog #30

"Mr. Monkey Porcupine"

I almost omitted this chapter from my book; the title alone could easily raise more than enough eyebrows. But as I thought more and more about it while putting these words to paper, I remembered that this was one of the more crazy dating experiences I had to date. And if this was something that I had experienced, and you are walking with me on this crazy journey that is my dating life, you should have the pleasure of experiencing it as well.

I met this guy on Match.com about a year after my move to Chicago, and while we did not have what I would consider a huge connection, he seemed nice enough and I was being open. After a short email session and a quick phone call, I made plans to meet him at Chicago's Hubbard Inn the following Friday night. I had finally gotten to the age where my weekends were not necessarily taken up by wild nights out drinking, and often times a Friday night consisted of me curled up on the couch, watching the shows I had missed earlier in the week. Having a first date on a Friday was no longer as strange as it had once been.

When I arrived at the bar, I saw my date already sipping a cocktail. I gave him a hug while I tried to take him in — Did he look like his picture? Check. Was he as tall as he said he was? Check. Okay, we were in business. I sat down and ordered a drink.

Eighty-second dating lesson learned: Just because a guy looked as he was supposed to, did not mean he would act as he was supposed to.

As we got to talking, I realized very quickly this guy had been through a lot in life — he had lost both of his parents at a young age, did not have siblings or any aunts/uncles, and was pretty much a loner. As a result, he was also a downer, maybe even depressed, and quite possibly an alcoholic. I knew pretty early on that he was not the one for me but I felt bad for him. When he told me the story of losing both of his parents my heart broke. So instead of pulling my "I'm tired" trick, and against my better judgment, I stuck it out.

After his ninth drink to my one (and that is by no means an exaggeration), he grabbed a napkin from the bar and asked the bartender for a pen. He told me we were going to play a game. I love games so I was hopeful maybe I would still be able to have a little fun.

He handed me the pen and said, "Please draw what it would look like if a monkey and a porcupine had sex and had a baby." Um this was interesting to say the least. It was a strange request and definitely did not feel very "game like," but I was a sucker for brainteasers and thought this had to be one of those. Now, understand going in that my artwork was far from Picasso. Heck, it was far from a good stick figure. But I did my best and drew the picture, kind of hiding it behind my hand so that no one else sitting at the bar would see it.

I handed it to my date and waited patiently for the big punch line that I believed was coming. Instead I was met with a long awkward silence as he took time to stare at my drawing. I sat there with a clock going in my head, tic tock, tic tock, tic tock. I felt like I was on Jeopardy during the final round, waiting for the buzzer to go off. As he continued to look at the napkin, I turned my attention to the TV screen in the bar that had one of the March Madness games on.

FINALLY, after what seemed like a decade, he looked back at me and spoke.

"Nice job."

That was it?! After all of that, that was it — nice job?! How was this a game or even a brainteaser? What was the point of me putting to paper the image of what would happen if a monkey and a porcupine elected to start copulating?

I was completely confused and really did not know what to say other than, "There's nothing else to this game?"

He simply looked back at me and said, "No."

I turned away from him for a second and took a long sip of my drink, contemplating if I should make up an excuse to make a run for it. The answer was so obvious and yet I could not bring myself to do it because I felt bad for this guy. Now I know that you should never stay on a date out of pity. It was a fruitless exercise and a waste of time for the person who knows there is no shot of a second date. It can give false hope to the other person across the table (Think Jim Carey in Dumb and Dumber: "So you're saying there's a CHANCE!"), and yet I stayed out with him for another two hours.

To this day, I cannot rationalize or understand my choice. He slammed back another five drinks to my one in that timeframe, and needless to say he was bombed. He had also started to get touchy feely and slur inappropriate things. It was all going downhill, and fast. I kept my body turned away from his, and stayed until the end of the basketball game. But the second the last point was scored and the time clock hit 0:00, I was out.

I tried to make the goodbye quick and painless, but my date/art critic/drunk was not having it. I told him I could easily get a cab on my own, but he insisted on walking (or I should say stumbling) me to the corner, all the while pleading his case to give him a second chance. I truly felt awful; this guy clearly had a tough life and was just a product of what he had been through.

Eighty-third dating lesson learned: Just because I believed in giving to charitable causes did not mean that applied to ALL aspects of my life. There was no such thing as charitable dating for a reason.

When a cab finally pulled up, I took a deep breath, put my sympathetic feelings aside and hugged him good-bye. It was not pretty. He continued to plead his case for a second date, even after I started to get in to the cab. I just had to shut it out of my mind and hope, for his sake, that he got some therapy and even checked himself in to Alcoholics Anonymous.

As soon as I slammed that cab door shut, wherever *Mr. Monkey Porcupine* ended up was no longer my concern. Dating someone out of sympathy certainly was not something I was about to start doing. Nor was it my duty or concern to help someone I met one time.

What was my concern was the fact that I had yet another notch of a failed dating attempt etched into my belt.

Frog #31

"Mr. Alcharexic"

I had never heard of an alcharexic until I dated one. And I can say that after the experience, I never ever wanted to meet another one again.

It was the fall of 2011. I had just gotten back from a nice trip to Paris with my friend Nikki; a trip that concurrently allowed me to also spend some time with my family that lives there, so I returned to the States feeling happy and at peace after a fulfilling vacation. As I played catch up, reading through all of the emails I had missed while I was out of the country, I came across a message from a new guy on Match.com. While he thought he was out of my age range (which was actually untrue — I just had not updated my profile, and therefore preferred age, in a while), he said I intrigued him because he loved that I traveled. He wanted to just tell me that and wished me luck in my search. I took a look at his pictures and he was very attractive — scratch that, he was hot. With his shaved head, round face, tanned body, huge blue eyes, and what appeared to be a model like body; I was nearly salivating at my computer screen. I read his profile, which focused a great deal on all of the exotic traveling he had done. I was definitely intrigued as I had been bitten by my own travel bug in my late 20's, and anyone who shared in my passion had a leg up on others right from the get go.

With that, I wrote him back and we immediately developed a great email rapport.

After one week of chatting with this guy, I knew this was going to turn in to something more than just a one-time date. I knew our first date would be a lot of fun. I knew I would want to see him again. I knew simply from my chapters and chapters of experience. When Marissa asked if I was nervous a few hours before I was supposed to meet him for the first time, I mocked her a little and said, "Are you nervous going to work every day?" At that, she laughed. Hard. But was it funny? I was not so sure. This was what dating had seemingly become to me — it really was a job. Ten-plus years in to it, I was no longer nervous anymore. Much like I no longer feared giving presentations in front of clients, going out on a first date had become something I could do very easily.

As predicted, my new guy and I went out. We had a really fun time. We got drunk, were touchy feely, laughed, got deep in conversation and made out. What more could you want from a first date?

He did however suggest something a little different for our second date, which drew me to him even more — he wanted to have a picnic with wine, cheese, crackers, fruits, etc. in Millennium Park so we could listen to the music that played there on Monday nights. Not only did this sound fun to me, but it also was a unique and romantic idea. I mean how many second dates were just "Which bar do you want to meet at and have a few cocktails?" He had put some thought in to this, and it definitely was a turn on that he had suggested doing something a little out of the box.

Eighty-fourth dating lesson learned: Even when all signs point to the positive, do not ever underestimate when a red flag will wave and say hello.

The first "red flag" wave came just shortly after he suggested this amazing date. He told me he would be taking the train in to the city from the burbs (ok, fine) but it was because he lived there… with his parents! While he explained it was to support them after his dad lost his job, I should have inquired more as to why a 41 year old could not just give them money versus feel the need to live with them. But I didn't; instead, I chose to see this as a positive in regards to his character.

Because of his "trek" on the train, he apparently did not want to lug all of the food and drinks onto the Metra. While I figured we could have easily gone together once he got to the city, he asked if I would go to the grocery store ahead of time and take care of it because he "didn't want to waste any time."

Really? He couldn't at the very least contribute to the picnic <u>he</u> so nicely suggested?

After a few seconds of feeling aggravated, the voices I had heard too many times in the last few years crept in: "You're not going to get everything. There are things you will need to compromise on." Maybe the compromise here was that he came up with cool/different ideas that were more exciting than the norm…but perhaps I would have to be the one to execute them? So with that thinking, I ignored that red flag number two.

Eighty-fifth dating lesson learned: You have to find a way to shut off the loud voices of others and listen to your more quiet voice buried below them.

We met at the train station, where I had the fruits, veggies, cheese and wine in tow…mind you it was still about a 10-block walk to the park and then another block or so to get to the spot where we were going to hang for the evening. One would have assumed he would have offered to carry at least a couple of the four bags I was holding. Nope. Instead, I got not one lift of a finger from a guy who had muscles that put Arnold Schwarzenegger in his hay day to shame.

And there was red flag number three, bigger and brighter than ever.

Still, I took a deep breath and decided to enjoy the lovely evening we had in store. We had amazingly perfect weather, good music, good food and I was with a really hot guy, someone so attractive that I actually felt a tiny bit uncomfortable. This guy had not one inch of fat on his body, and making out with him, I could not help but run my hands over his stomach and back — it was like nothing I had ever felt before. In plain English, he was ripped.

Somehow that fact, mixed in with his amazing blue eyes, led me to overlook the biggest red flag yet — I was the only one who ate that evening. Sure the alcohol was downed by both of us, but I had eaten the fruit, cheese and crackers all by myself. Instead of giving that some credence, I decided to ignore the facts and dove directly in to his abs, I mean arms, for the next few weeks with nothing but excitement.

After all, who cared if this guy was not a gentleman, or he was bunking with his parents in the burbs, or I never saw him eat? No big deal. He was gorgeous and kept me laughing and THAT was what mattered, right? With that rationale, I continued to date the guy.

Eighty-sixth dating lesson learned: Red flags are red for a reason. Just like stop signs, or red lights, you are not supposed ignore them or disaster could ensue.

We made a dinner date for the Tuesday after the weekend I went to visit my sister in Austin, Texas. After all of the fried chicken and barbecue I had just stuffed myself with, I suggested we grab sushi. I needed to return to some lighter, healthier dining.

He met me at my apartment and we walked over to the restaurant. Halfway there he randomly asked what I had eaten for lunch. I was not sure why this was interesting to him, but I indulged and said "A salad and some potato chips." Silence. Was I now supposed to ask him what he had eaten? I really didn't care but when the silence ensued, I felt compelled to indulge him, "And what did you have?"

And there it was. THE moment. The moment everything changed, and I got out of his abs and back in to my right mind.

"I had three egg whites. That is all I eat every day for lunch during the week. I need to save my calories for alcohol."

I had to process that for a minute because I could not comprehend what he had just said to me.

"So all you eat is egg whites for lunch to save calories?" "What about dinner?" I figured this was somewhat important considering we were but moments away from sitting down to eat.

"Oh yeah," he responded. "I don't eat dinner during the week."

I was officially blown away. He doesn't eat dinner during the week? Well no freaking wonder why this guy did not have an ounce of fat on him! Honestly, how did I find these guys?

"But we are going to dinner," I noted. "Are you just going to watch me eat?"

Very matter-of-factly he replied, "Yeah. Maybe I'll get a little appetizer, but I'm not really going to eat."

And there it was - I was dating an alcharexic. By definition, this was a person who "saves" calories by not eating so that they can drink more alcohol and still maintain their physique.

Eighty-seventh Dating Lesson Learned: Sushi is not seen as healthier eating to someone who is an alcharexic.

I had a decision to make. Did I end things right then and go home to eat in peace without feeling like I was the crazy one for wanting and needing dinner? Or did I go through with this date because I was starving and we had arrived at the restaurant? I went with the latter, but in hindsight, I would have been better off with the former.

Dinner was good for me in that I ordered the rolls I had been craving and they were delicious. Dinner was bad for me because *Mr. Alcharexic* ordered an appetizer that was no bigger than four peanuts. There was nothing worse than going to dinner with someone but feeling like you were eating alone. For all of you single ladies out there, if you date an alcharexic, it means you will be dining alone quite often. I do not care how hot a guy is, it was absolutely not worth it.

Just when I was sure things could not have gotten any worse, they did. The check arrived, and *Mr. Alcharexic* turned to me and literally said, "Do you have $5 for the tip? Oh wait no you're a chick. You would never have $5 on you, and if you did you'd pretend you didn't."

That was the final straw. There were so many things that were wrong with the evening. And if I chose not to see the big huge red neon flags waving in front of my nose now, any hope for me was certainly lost.

Luckily I did.

So I did what I knew I needed to do and I ended the relationship with *Mr. Alcharexic*. The best part was he claimed he had been feeling the same way, but in the same breath asked what I meant when I told him point blank that, "there were things that made me realize we aren't compatible."

I do not think this guy was used to girls breaking up with him. I think he was usually the one who did the breaking. However, his ego was not my problem, nor my concern.

We did remain "friends" on Facebook, and every so often his posts would show up in my news feed. He would only post pictures of himself, and his muscles, in weird places all over the world (very remote places in Africa where indigenous people live) that he often visited. Not that I needed it, but it continued to validate the choice I had made to walk away from him and this relationship.

I just hated that once again another break up was the right decision...

Frog #32

"Mr. Tattoo"

The New Year had arrived and with it I was ready for something new. I had taken a brief three-month hiatus from dating after the *Mr. Alcharexic* craziness and was ready to get back on the dating bandwagon. Many of you reading this have to be thinking by now "Jesus lady, why don't you just throw in the towel already? Its clear love is not in your cards in this lifetime!" But what could I say? I was, and always have been, a glutton for punishment. Even more than that, I was not ready to give up on that deep, intense, unconditional love I was looking for.

Melissa, one of my closest friends in Chicago, had just become "official" with Jesse, the guy she had been dating for about 2 months. I adored her new boyfriend and as luck would have it, he had "a great single Jewish friend" they wanted to set me up with. I was thrilled about this, especially because it was a set up. I was so over online dating where I seemed to only be meeting total losers, alcharexics or it was heartbreak hotel. Set ups allowed for information to be relayed and at the very least, the guy had to be somewhat decent as he was a friend of the same friends I had chosen. As per the usual, my number was given out and we made plans to meet up the following week.

Our first date was at Sushi Samba where we ended up having a great time. We talked about everything and anything from our jobs and families to how much personal work we had each done on ourselves. He had been married, had a kid, and was now divorced all within a two year period. I will admit I was initially hesitant about going out with him after Melissa had told me about his "situation" (kids can often add a more complicated element when dating was often complicated enough). But as he and I got to know each other that evening, he talked a lot about how ready he was for that real deal relationship. We both agreed we were completely over the wounded birds and general head cases we had each seemed to be meeting. That night, we both appeared ready, willing, and able to find that something special. It was so refreshing to hear so any trepidation I had about his past was put to bed. I was excited to connect with someone who seemed to be on my same level.

Eighty-eighth dating lesson learned: People can present themselves any way they want on a first date. They may truly want to be the person they say they are, but reality may sometimes differ.

Because we had such an easy first date, and because we had the benefit of our closest friends giving us feedback, the relationship took off. We texted pretty much every day right from that point on and made plans for a second date. I kept saying that this was how it was supposed to be. No drama. No games. No analyzing… just easy. I could not see this going anywhere other than to a good place.

Shortly in to our relationship we decided to make dinner plans with the amazing friends that had set us up. While we were still very much in the "getting to know you" phase (usually the period of time when you do things alone with one another), our comfort level had grown at such an accelerated pace that it didn't feel awkward to be double dating yet. In fact, it felt just the opposite; it was very natural and comfortable. And that ease eventually continued back in my apartment where we had a two-hour make out session. He confessed how much he liked me and I felt my heart melt a bit. Was this all too good to be true?

Later that same weekend, I had made plans to watch Sunday football with the girls at a local bar. My new guy wanted to see me again and asked if he could join after he dropped his daughter off at his ex-wife's house. I was more than pleasantly surprised he wanted to see me again so soon after our last date, so I said "Of course, come hang out!"

He arrived at the bar a few minutes in to the first game and just chilled with the girls and me. I loved that he seemed to be up for anything just so he could see me; I knew a lot of guys who may have refused to sit in a bar with a group of girls all afternoon. However, he was eventually afforded some "man relief" when Jesse and Melissa showed up after half time.

About halfway through the second game he and I decided we were both a little tired and wanted some alone time, so we said our good-byes and headed out, arm in arm. We stopped to get chocolate-covered strawberries (both of our favorites) and then headed back to my apartment to watch the end of the game. We curled up on the couch but noticed the halftime show was still going on, which incidentally we both found to be far from entertaining. So we decided to make our own entertainment, which was easy enough to do… first on the couch, and then eventually made our way in to the bedroom.

As things heated up, my shirt came off which exposed him to the little red rose tattoo I have on my lower left side. And it was in that exact moment when everything just stopped; the palpable change was overwhelming and I actually felt the energy in the room shift. As he examined the ink on my skin, I was suddenly tangled up in the most extreme bug out moment I had ever witnessed.

"You have a tattoo?" he asked, as if I was Mother Theresa and he could not imagine how someone in that vein could have a tattoo. He put extra emphasis on the "you", which only amplified the situation. As I confirmed what seemed to be his worst nightmare (the fact I even had to confirm it was unreal to me. The ink was there on my skin. What the hell else could it have been?), he again regurgitated his sentiment, "I just can't believe YOU have a tattoo!"

I was not sure what to say other than "Yes, I have a tattoo." Was this guy serious? I could not even tell you how many men had seen this tattoo and not blinked an eye. But with his reaction, you would have thought having ink was the equivalent to confessing to murder.

It was really awkward.

The worst part — I had a second tattoo. While it was only a little ladybug the size of a pea on my foot, I spent the next 60 seconds having an internal debate with myself as to whether or not I should tell *Mr. Tattoo*. Doing so may well have thrown him into a complete state of shock and I definitely did not want him to have a heart attack in my apartment; I opted to keep it to myself.

We made our way back out to the living room to watch the rest of the football game. There was zero doubt that things had gotten strange between us, but I did my best to ignore it and have a good time. I was doing a decent job until he took my un-socked feet, put them on his legs and looked down. I cringed knowing full well what was coming next was not going to be anything good.

Eighty-ninth dating lesson learned: If you attempt to hide the tattoo on your foot, you should be advised to wear socks.

"You have <u>another</u> tattoo?" he asked, in an even more shocked tone than after discovering the first one. He then followed up with an accusatory, "What ELSE don't I know about you?"

How was I supposed to even answer that question? There were a lot of things he didn't know about me yet, but that shouldn't have meant I had now become a person who was hiding deep dark secrets, did it? I had many men in my life who had seen my tattoo's and did not blink an eye at them, so it had never occurred to me that this was information I should thought to have divulged on date one. I wasn't keeping it from him; I just simply never thought it would have been such an issue. There was part of me that wanted to point all of this out to him, but I knew in my heart of hearts that the train had completely left the tracks and there was no hope for it to re-rail. I knew in that moment, and from the way he reacted, whatever it was that had started between us was now over.

He left my apartment only a few minutes after that last horribly uncomfortable exchange and I immediately called Melissa to tell her that the fairytale she had of the four of us vacationing together in the Virgin Islands was no longer in the cards. She literally thought I was nuts, noting that she had just seen us together and that "we looked so cute."

I replied very matter-of-factly, "I'm aware. But what just transpired in my apartment a few minutes ago was not something that was going to lead to a long-term relationship. I think we both need to come to the realization that we are not going to be marrying best friends."

She had been single long enough to know the gut feeling I was referring to, but after seeing us just a few hours prior she absolutely could not comprehend any of it. I couldn't blame her; I was still in shock myself.

But the reality was, I was a dating veteran and had been doing this way too long to not know the certainty of the situation I was in. It was too bad there were no gold medals or lifetime achievement awards in the world of dating. I swore with the experiences, knowledge, and pure instincts I had under my belt, I could have won five times over by then.

So while Melissa maintained hope, I waited for the truth to come out…And waited…And waited some more. I initially assumed he would have told me when he called to let me know he had gotten home ok like I had asked him to do. But no. A call never came in that Sunday night, nor did it come in Monday or Tuesday. It was days of waiting before I would finally be given confirmation that my instincts on that momentous evening had been spot on.

And this was once again where I did not understand men. He knew whatever we might have had relationship-wise was dead and gone. He knew the moment he left my apartment. But he decided it would be a good idea to wait three days before he called to tell me how he was feeling. Three days. Three whole days! We had been speaking or in touch every day up until that point, so to go seventy-two hours with zero contact did not really leave much mystery as to what was going on. Why not just end it in my apartment? Or call later on that night? Or as a last resort the next day? And yes, I could have called him but whatever pride I had left stood in the way of allowing myself to lend a helping hand. So instead, I waited for him to call me, festering with my own thoughts, and growing angrier and angrier in response to his delayed action; it was nothing short of selfish.

Typically girls tend to not make our feelings known, or are not so obvious with how we feel, until we are ready to end it. Our actions don't switch from one side of the coin to the other in a matter of minutes and then not address it for days upon days. If men could learn to provide the same courtesy I believed it would be much appreciated by most, if not all women. Something I would add to the Dating 101 course I was beginning to think I should conduct for this group of our species.

When I received the insider information (aka Melissa told me) that he would finally be contacting to me to talk, I went to my friend Erica's apartment for dinner so I did not have to be alone when the dreaded phone call came in. But to be honest, I no longer had any interest in speaking to him. I was beyond annoyed and had zero interest in hearing him say what I already knew he would. I could have written the script on my own so why did I have to hear it come out of his mouth when I had known for days it was over?

If it had not been for Erica, I honestly don't think I would have taken his call that night. She nearly grabbed the phone out of my hand to hit the "answer" button on my cell because she knew I needed to just get it over with.

I ended up doing it myself, but only because I knew there was no way Erica was going to allow the call to go to voicemail.

I was immediately met with, "Hey Court what's up? How was your day?"

I had no interest in making small talk, especially with someone who had gone dark on me for three days. I was not shy in letting him know how I felt.

"I'm not really interested in chatting about my day," I told him directly. "Why don't you just get to the point?"

No exaggerating. That was my response. My patience for this nonsense had grown to be nonexistent. The "I'm so in to you, but I'm going to change my mind in a blink of an eye because something bugs me out" card had been played, and I was finished with it. And him.

"Okay Court. I'm sorry. I just think you're so amazing and so wonderful and … "

I literally stopped him mid-sentence. I could not take the "You are the most amazing thing on earth, so cool, fun and smart, but I don't want to date you" spiel. I could not take that conversation, because it was a load of crap. Just simply be honest, say how you felt about not wanting to date me, and call it a day. The fluff just made it a million times worse. I knew how great I was. I didn't need him telling me.

However, what I DID want to discuss was the fact that I felt duped by him. I wanted him to explain how he could be so in to me just moments before he discovered I had a tattoo. I wanted him to admit that the element of surprise had freaked him out. I wanted him to admit that he freaked out in general; that things had moved quickly, and while it was easy, it was scary for him. That it was not that he did not want to date me per se, but that in truth, he was not really ready for a relationship with anyone. That he was not capable at this point of truly giving over his feelings or his heart after his divorce. And that even though he believed he was, he actually was not. I wanted and needed that validation because everything in my gut told me this was the truth. But of course I would not get it.

Until I did…

A friend of mine ended up dating *Mr. Tattoo* a few years later, but for much longer - a year and a half to be exact. She was invested. She was committed. She made many changes to her life for him. She was in love. And watching them together, we all believed he was too. But in what felt like a blink of an eye, he stripped her of it all, of course not before he made grand gestures leading her to believe they would spend their lives together. He demonstrated his true lack of understanding of what it actually takes to be in a happy, successful relationship; seeing and hearing it as an outsider looking in, I had never been so sure of this being the truth as I was then. He believes he knows. He believes he tries. He believes he gives it his all. But believing you have the key and actually physically having the key are two very different things.

Helping her through those initial days after their break up left me feeling three distinct emotions: incredibly sad (for her heart break), very happy (for me and the bullet I dodged), and unfortunately validated (for not wanting to have been right for her sake, but now knowing I was).

It was after my own experience with *Mr. Tattoo* that I reached a point where I actually started to wonder if I should continue to put myself out there the way I had for the last nine years. Whether I felt bad because I had to break it off with someone because they were not Mr. Right for me, or someone else broke it off with me because I was not Ms. Right for them, it was all getting tired. And so was I. Was this roller coaster of emotional craziness all worth it? Would it be easier if I just threw in the towel and maintained being status quo — sure there would be no ups, but then again would it not also mean there would be no downs?

This was something I had seriously begun to contemplate.

Frog #'s 33 & 34

"Mr. VacationS"

When I moved to Chicago, I hit the jackpot in the friend department. I was so lucky to have met so many amazing new people, but there were five girls in particular with whom I formed a very deep bond – we not only had a ton of fun all together, but we were truly there for each other when it came to being each other's sounding board when it came to everything and anything from work to family and of course to dating. The six of us had all been through enough with the opposite sex that if I had compiled all of their stories with mine, we might have been looking at a 1,000-page novel. Lucky for all of you, we spared you and stuck to mine alone.

Within this nice group we had formed, I shared different interests with each of the girls that I loved and appreciated. For example, Erica and I both had a love for food and trying new restaurants. She was also who I could spend hours on the phone with analyzing every date or feeling either of us had about any given guy we were going out with. Melissa and I loved bike riding on the lake and would often meet one time a week to go for a ride after work, marveling at the amazing city we lived in. Aubrey shared my obsession with massages and spas; we would go for reflexology any chance we could. During a trip we took to Cabo, we found a 90 minute massage for $25 and went EVERY DAY. Nikki and I were both in love with Paris and speaking French; we went as far as conducting our own French course (class of two) on the living room floor of my apartment. And last, but certainly far from least, Alana and I bonded over our love for traveling; we could go anywhere and do anything as long as it was an adventure and a new place to see and experience. The first time I met Alana, we both talked extensively about how we had a strong desire to go to South America and wanted to start with Argentina. Initially she was planning on going with a friend of hers from college, but when those plans fell through, she was looking for someone else to go with her. I quickly, and very happily, stepped in… and with that, I found my South American Travel Buddy.

Within a year, we managed to go on two big trips together — one to Argentina, which included Buenos Aires, Mendoza and Bariloche; and the second to Chile, which included Atacama, Santiago, Puerta Natales and Valparaiso. We did not rely on a travel agent, but instead did all of the planning on our own. I was really proud of us for putting together such amazing trips, not to mention, we afforded them straight from our own hard-earned money. These were, and will always remain, experiences that I am truly thankful for; had I found my Mr. Right earlier in my life, I may not have had the chance to have them.

With all of the adventures Alana and I created for ourselves in both countries: remarkable sites, immersing in the cultures, partying, eating like queens, wine tasting, shopping, hiking, biking, kayaking, white-water rafting, horseback riding, and tanning on the beach, we could not leave out meeting guys. I mean what was a vacation without a hot hook-up?

Both of our trips were made complete when we met guys who were both charming and very easy on the eyes. These vacation hook-ups were the perfect way to feel attractive, let loose, and not worry about a thing except to have fun. They were a short glimpse in to what it was like to have a boyfriend for a few days, without actually having to deal with the commitment or baggage that comes from entering in to a relationship.

I acknowledged that when I was home in my everyday routine, I would often spend a lot time longing for that special relationship. I wanted to find my true love and thought about it quite a bit. But when I was on vacation, my mind felt free. There was no worrying about my age, where my friends were in their lives versus where I was, or that I was alone — nope, there was only a feeling of complete gratitude for each and every experience I was having and enjoying every second of it. There were no consequences or judgment. It was on these trips where I was able to 100% live in the moment. And while it was like I was escaping reality for a week or so, I felt I deserved that. It was what would get me through the monotony I felt at times in my everyday life back in the States.

Enter Mr. Vacation Number One

On the first night of our trip to Argentina, we were out in Buenos Aires and ended up at a local bar. It was just what we wanted because it was our mission to immerse ourselves in the culture, and not seem "American". Within five minutes, Alana spotted a cute group of guys and decided to approach them. It should be noted that on vacation there was no fear of approaching cute guys — that was non-existent on vacation.

"Hola!" she said to the tallest of the bunch, trying out her most South American Spanish accent.

She was met with, "You American?"

Feeling a bit disenchanted that our plan to not seem "American" had backfired quickly Alana gave a humble nod in response. Luckily he was very excited we were from the States with his, "Awesome! I'm from Cali!" and the next thing we knew, we had made new friends in Buenos Aires. We quickly got over the fact that they were "just American" and spent the rest of our time in BA partying with them.

There was no such thing as sleeping in this town. For anyone who not had the good fortune to go there, it is customary to sit down to dinner at 11pm followed by dancing the night away until 7am. The first night we came back to our hotel at 3:30am and the young guy at the concierge mocked our "early arrival", stating he "was just getting ready to go out for the night!"

We quickly adapted by night two and found ourselves out with the California Boys until 7am. We partied with them until we coupled off, I with my *Mr. Vacation Number One*. While sweet and funny, physically he was not my type. He was shorter and stockier than I typically went for and his entire back and majority of his arms were covered in large tattoos. He looked like one of the guys cast in the "Jersey Shore" but it truly made no difference to me. I wasn't marrying the guy; heck after my night out with him came to an end, I knew I was likely never going to see him. So I enjoyed myself to the max and the trip was proving to be nothing short of perfection!

Ninetieth dating lesson learned: Every single girl must experience vacation sex at least once. It is a no strings attached pleasure that is well deserved.

Of course all good things must often come to an end. The morning it was time for us to head to Mendoza, we tried to sneak out of the guys' apartment without waking them. Both of us agreed there was no need for sappy good-byes or "keep in touches." As far as we were concerned, we had a blast and now it was time to move on.

There was only one problem with this escape plan. We were locked in.

As we tried to execute a covert operation to exit the premises, we literally could not get their front door open for anything. We tried everything — pushing, pulling, a various number of keys that were on the coffee table next to their random friend who had passed out half-naked with ink painted on his face by yours truly — but nothing was working. To make things worse, I could not see a thing as I had to take out my contacts and put them in cups of water for the two hours I attempted to sleep, which was not a smart idea.

Note to self: when hooking up, try to find someone who wore contacts so that there was a guarantee of saline solution available.

It was literally the blind leading the blind, and what we had planned to execute as a quick getaway turned in to one of the funniest moments of our trip. Eventually, with all of our effort and clamoring, we made enough noise the guys had no choice but to come downstairs. Of course they "rescued" us with ease, but not before calling us out for trying to leave without a proper good-bye.

Ninety-first dating lesson learned: Vacation sex was all about channeling your inner-Samantha Jones via Sex and The City. She was a one and done kind of gal and you could be too… on vacation.

While we never saw those guys again, we did keep in touch on Facebook. And if we ever found ourselves on the West Coast, we knew we had hot friends to call.

Enter Mr. Vacation Number Two

One year later, almost to the day, Alana and I were on our second adventure. This time the destination was Chile and we had planned ahead, making friends in Santiago before we even left the States. And when I say "friends," I mean ridiculously good-looking guys that lived there. We arranged to meet up with them when we arrived so that they could take us round and "show us a good time."

And a good time was exactly what we had!

Our first night out in Santiago was a double date for dinner, where I formally met *Mr. Vacation Number Two* in person. Up until that point, we had formed an email relationship, but in person, he was nothing short of hot and sexy in a very "South American" way, although admittedly he was originally from Puerto Rico, but what did it matter? He had a sexy accent, beautifully tanned skin, black piercing eyes that felt like they had the ability to see right through me, and a smile that could melt anyone's heart; I actually felt giddy around him. So when he made the move to passionately kiss me on the dance floor of the club he and his friend had taken us to, my knees nearly buckled and I was in "vacation love."

As most vacation hook-ups typically went, we became instant boyfriend/girlfriend. We looked like we were a couple for years in any and every picture we took over the next six hours. The timing could not have been better as this was about two weeks after *Mr. Tattoo* had abruptly ended things with me. I was excited to post the pictures of my hot new South American/Puerto Rican boyfriend on Facebook where I secretly hoped the tattoo man would see them and maybe feel a twinge of jealousy. Oh the mindless games we sometimes played with ourselves…typically silly and pointless, but in the moment they really do appear to be the perfect "revenge" plan.

While we had to leave the next day for Puerto Natales, which was literally at the end of the earth and very far away from my new "boyfriend", Alana and I had already planned to head back to Santiago later in the week for round two. So I spent the next few days flirting with *Mr. Vacation Number Two* via Blackberry Messenger until we were reunited.

And reunite, we did!

Our second night out in Santiago was even better than the first. The guys took us to a swanky bar we would have never found on our own where we ate, drank and partied like it was 1999. I was having a blast and at that moment could not think of any other place in the world I would rather be. Finding Mr. Right? Eh, whatever! I had found Mr. Right Now and I was in "vacation heaven." As we headed back to his place late night, we made out like crazy; I could not keep my hands off of this guy. To my surprise, I found myself actually feeling sad that I had to leave the next day and would most likely never see him again.

Ninety-second dating lesson learned: It was possible to "fall" for your Mr. Vacation. While it certainly was not encouraged, it could happen. My inner-Samantha Jones had turned in to my inner-Charlotte York.

This was <u>not</u> supposed to be happening. Vacation sex was supposed to equal no feelings, just fun. But somehow, I found *Mr. Vacation Number Two* to be so sweet, smart and appealing that the idea of leaving was making me feel down and uneasy. Unfortunately, there was not a damn thing I could do about it. My plane back to reality was leaving on the last day of February and not being on it was absolutely not an option.

Ninety-third dating lesson learned: Denial was a very easy way to make unwanted feelings go away.

So I did what any "normal" girl should do if she found herself in the same situation — I pretended that I would see *Mr. Vacation Number Two* in a few months when he came to visit me in Chicago. Yep. I decided that was the plan and I was sticking to it. When I returned State side, we kept in touch via our blackberry instant messenger, and I convinced myself he would eventually confirm his flight number and the days he would be staying with me.

My made up fantasy is what got me through the next few weeks once I was back to the real world. And by the time *Mr. Vacation Number Two* was "scheduled" to visit me, according to my made-up story, he had become but a distant memory — a blast from the past that I had fond memories of, but whom I was completely over.

Ninety-fourth dating lesson learned: "Out of sight, out of mind" really is a very true statement.

And that was what *Mr. Vacations* were for. Whether it be a hot hook up you just have fun with or a crush you fantasize about when you got home — no matter the case, it was a win/win for any single girl and something I strongly encourage all of you out there to find on your next trip.

Frog #35

"Mr. Hookah"

It was mid-March 2012 and I was out with a few friends at a bar watching March Madness. We were just chilling, having a few drinks and watching some college basketball when I spotted this really hot guy across the bar. We made eye contact a few times and I could not stop looking at him. It had gotten to the point where I wished I was wearing an invisibility cloak from Harry Potter because I was embarrassing myself with the number of stares I was giving.

Ninety-fifth dating lesson learned: You are not embarrassing yourself if he was looking back at you. It meant he was doing exactly the same thing.

The next thing I knew, he and his friends had made their way over to the area where I was standing. We ended up back to back and I felt my heart racing. I wanted to turn around so badly and start a conversation but what was I going to say? Was it not the guy's job to initiate a conversation? Wasn't there some rule written down somewhere in all of those dating/relationship self-help books I had spent much of my earlier days reading that talked about this very subject? Hadn't I been led to believe when it came to dating, the golden rule of thumb was letting the man be the man?

However, holding back had gotten be nowhere to date; it was time for me to do things differently. So after a few deep breaths, and some hemming and hawing, I decided to do the boldest thing I had done to date. I went up to the bar, got a napkin and asked for a pen.

I wrote my name and number down, folded it up and marched my way back to the guy I had not been able to take my eyes off. I tapped him on the shoulder and said "Hi, I'm Courtney. I think you're really cute. I know you are hanging with your friends tonight, as am I, but here's my number. If you're interested, call me." I handed him the napkin, turned around and walked away.

I was on a total high! I had completely forgotten about what was to happen next — whether or not he called suddenly became irrelevant. I was simply proud of myself for having the guts to do something like that for the first time in my life — and sober too! My friends were impressed and I could leave the bar with a smile on my face.

Ninety-sixth dating lesson learned: Men desire confidence in the opposite sex. They spend enough of their time approaching girls and getting rejected. Any help we provide in this department is welcomed and appreciated.

And wouldn't you know, the next day I got a text asking me out for the following Thursday! I may have done a small victory dance in my apartment before sending a mass email, gloating to all of my friends.

When he picked me up in a cab on the night of our first date, he looked amazing. He was dressed really well in nice dark jeans, a button down, and a burgundy sweater. The color went great with his dark hair and complexion. While he did not have an accent, I quickly learned he was fluent in Spanish as it was his first language. There was something about these Latino men lately; I was very drawn to them in a way that made my insides tingle.

After a fifteen-minute ride, we arrived at the Hookah Lounge (hence his name) he had chosen for our first date. I will say that while it was a dating first, it was a very cool experience, and one I encourage everyone to do at least once. We selected our flavors, sat on these colorful pillows on the ground, and smoked away. We talked about life and got in to some deep conversations about the world and how much technology has evolved in the last few years. We spent a good three hours in the Hookah Lounge before heading back to my apartment where we had the longest and honestly best make-out session I may have ever had; the chemistry was unreal. When it was finally time for him to leave, he said he could not wait to see me again, and asked if we could meet up over the weekend.

To say I was on Cloud 9 would be an understatement. I had met this amazingly cute guy, on my own accord, landed a date with him, had an awesome time on the date, had great physical chemistry and he wanted to see me again that weekend?!

For the first half of the following week, I was on a total high. I had done the most daring thing I had ever done in my dating life — and it had paid off! I bragged to anyone and everyone about my boldness. Which also meant everyone and anyone continued to ask for updates.

This was not great when I did not have one to share.

By Thursday, when I still had not heard from *Mr. Hookah*, I started to wonder, "Was this going to be another *Mr. McShady* blow off?" I tried to not let my brain go in that direction because I just could not see this guy being a douche bag, but then again, I could not be a fool. I had too much experience under my belt to know by now that guys were capable of anything, no matter what the initial impression may have been.

When Saturday rolled around I knew there would be no weekend date. But I was totally and completely stumped as to why. I called Marissa to tell her about the situation. After nearly ten years of being on this roller coaster with me, she too had no words. I had left one of the most vocal, outspoken people I had ever known totally speechless. She could not make sense of it either, and so there we sat, in silence, just shaking our heads on both ends of the phone – from Chicago to NY.

On Sunday evening, the answer to my confusion came. And while it was not the answer I wanted, like "Oh my God, I'm so sorry I've been out of touch. I had a family emergency I had to tend to," or "Oh my God, I'm so sorry I've been out of touch. I lost my phone and didn't have your number for this past week", it was one that I could live with:

> *"Hey Court. I'm so sorry I've been out of touch. I just want to be honest and let you know that while I had a great time with you, and there was clearly something between us, that I was dating someone more casually up until this point. However, we had a talk this week and we are going to give this relationship a try, so I wanted to let you know and be straightforward. I didn't want to lead you on. I think you are great and please don't hate me."*

Hate him? Quite the contrary! Every guy on the planet should take a lesson from *Mr. Hookah*! That simple text made more than enough sense to me. I appreciated his honesty and the fact he took the time to acknowledge that we did have chemistry, that he did like me, but that he simply became exclusive with someone else.

Ninety-seventh dating lesson learned: Some good things do have to come to an end, even if you do not want them to.

In the end, this had nothing to do with me and had everything to do with poor timing. I could live with this. And I could not thank him enough for having the balls to be honest.

Ninety-eighth dating lesson learned: While I had not found Mr. Right, moving on from this form of "rejection" was very easy

Truth be told, I think this may be the dating story I was most proud of as it represented a distinct period in time where something had switched for me. I had my own inner confidence and went after what I wanted in a very authentic, true-to-myself way. I know…it only took me nine plus years!!

Frog #36

"Mr. Music"

In this book, I have used pseudonyms for the characters to protect myself (and them). They have been strategically tied to some type of outlandish behavior, idiosyncrasy, feature, or circumstance. But there was no way I could write this chapter without revealing the reason for the name had nothing to do with him being a musician. It was simply his last name and I loved it. My friends and I continue to refer to him by his first and last name as one name to this day. His name had such a ring to it and frankly, so did his persona. *Mr. Music* always managed to show up at the exact time when I needed him. I truly cannot say a bad word about the guy.

My first encounter with *Mr. Music* happened in March 2011. It was St. Patrick's Day in Chicago and my friends and I were in it for the long haul. As a side note, for those of you who have never been to Chicago on St. Patrick's Day, it was truly a sight to behold and an experience not to be forgotten. The whole city typically joined in on the festivities; a united drunken front and fun had by all!

That year, the party started at a friend's place in the Lakeview neighborhood and eventually made its way to a bar in Lincoln Park where the craziness ensued. After providing our ID's to the bouncers, we joined a group of guys playing flip cup (I often wondered if my college days were ever going to end), one of whom I noticed nearly immediately. He was tall, very cute, had light blonde hair, blue eyes, and a killer smile. I made my way over to his side of the table, and while the details of what happened next were a little hazy due to the heavy amounts of alcohol I had consumed, *Mr. Music* had somehow become my St Patty's Day boyfriend pretty quickly. We held hands, he rubbed my back and neck, always made sure I was ok, and got me a drink whenever I needed one. When his friends made the decision to move on to the next bar, he begged me to go with him — I loved every moment of it all.

The night ended with a very PG make-out session at my apartment, where he stayed until he had to leave for the airport to catch his flight. He was on his way back to the city where he had just moved – New York.

While it was a bummer *Mr. Music* didn't live in Chicago, the luck of the leprechaun was on my side, as I happened to be going to The Big Apple the very next weekend for my mom's birthday. Before he left, we exchanged numbers and made plans to see each other the following Saturday.

Who knew a St. Patty's Boyfriend could turn in to more than a one-night make out?

When I arrived in NY I was so excited to see *Mr. Music* again. While he had a work function that evening, his plan was for him to meet up the second he could escape from his professional duties. I waited patiently for three hours until he finally joined the party. By that point, I was actually exhausted and really just wanted to go back to his place for some alone time. Unfortunately he had nothing but lots of energy to burn off and had no intention of leaving the bar any time soon. Instead I was somewhat forced to stand by his side as he partied for another two hours.

Going in to that evening I knew things could move in one of two directions. The first was that he ended up being someone I really liked and we could actually decide to date long distance. The second left him as just a guy I met on St. Patty's Day, never to be seen again after that night.

We landed somewhere in the middle...

After spending the night with *Mr. Music* in NY, I knew we had amazing physical chemistry but it was very clear we were not only in very different spots in our lives (he was just beginning a new chapter in NY and I had zero intention of moving back there), we were also very different people. While he was a TON of fun, his level of energy never slowed. It was like he was on speed every moment of the day and I could not, nor did I have the desire to, keep up. So instead of becoming my next boyfriend, *Mr. Music* would be the man to save the day whenever I was in need of some good old-fashioned excitement; he would show up, deliver on my wants and desires, and then be on his way before he became too much for me to deal with.

Over the course of the next year he became my saving grace many a time. He would pop in — and pop out. Whether I happened to be in New York or he was in Chicago, we would always have a good time, but in between we would barely speak. Our "relationship" was based on an unspoken understanding, and it was one of the best gifts I had ever given myself. I could not have been happier when we would see each other, but I could only handle his level of energy for about 24 hours. Based on who and how he was, the amount of time we would spend together had become nothing short of perfection.

In June of 2012, *Mr. Music* once again showed up right when I required a much-needed dose of him. While I had discovered a new side of myself during the *Mr. Hookah* chapter, post that situation I had found myself in a dating lull, and had not found someone I liked since that time a few months prior. I was nearing my 35th birthday, and feeling like there was not a man in site that intrigued me as the middle of my decade arrived, left me feeling a bit down, discouraged, and not quite like myself.

But a little luck was on my side when I received a text from *Mr. Music* saying he was coming to Chicago for work in two days and would love to come hang out with me until his meeting at 6pm that evening. It was a no brainer.

"Hell yes *Mr. Music*…HELL YES!" was my response back to his request. While it was be just a shot versus the whole bottle of medicine I needed, the timing could not have been more perfect.

However, I should have remembered whom I was dealing with when he announced he was getting on a 6 a.m. flight and would be blowing in to my apt by 7:30 a.m.! Only *Mr. Music* would choose to fly in that early, and then show up rearing and ready to go. I had made breakfast for both of us but I watched him scarf his down within five minutes, all the while talking a mile a minute about God knows what. He was incapable of sitting still and I was exhausted just watching him. Was his high-speed personality a result of being on drugs? It was certainly a possibility, but I could care less. I knew I was going to get what I needed from him and had no interest in knowing or involving myself in anything else going on in his life.

Mr. Music always knew how to blow the smoke up my butt I needed right when I needed it. After an hour or two of sun bathing on my roof deck, where he offered up many compliments on how good I looked, we headed back to my bedroom for an afternoon of — well, fun. It was just what the Dr. had ordered; I felt like "Stella" in "Stella Got Her Groove Back". While we were not meant to be "forever" as Stella and Winston had been, and it would be the last time I'd ever see him, *Mr. Music* was exactly the jumpstart I needed to at least want to connect with a member of the opposite sex; he was somehow able to reignite the desire within me to get back on that dating bandwagon I had jumped off of for a bit, and for that I will always be thankful to him.

Ninety-ninth dating lesson learned: Every girl should get her groove back with her own version "Mr. Music". Every girl.

Frog #37

"Mr. Devil In The White City"

With just one week until my 35th birthday reared its ugly head, the anxiety had begun to build. I don't know why so many of us get caught up in a number, but at the end of the day, we just do. And for single women, this was especially true. It was like after a certain age, you heard that awful "tic-tock" sound in your head nonstop. And if it did stop, well not to worry, you had your family members to reset it.

There I was. Thirty-four years, 11 months, five days and single as single could be. While I preferred not to go back to online dating for the 3,294,083,243rd round, I knew that I needed to keep all options open and that no action would lead to zero reward. So once again I gave it the old college try. I upped my game on Match.com and let the influx of random emails begin.

While most of the correspondences I received were not even worth mentioning, there was one guy who stood out. He was fun, sarcastic and witty, and we had amazing banter. It was exactly the kind I always craved and found so hard to find. We spent a week straight texting non-stop and I knew I would at least have a good time on a date with this guy. When he finally asked me out, I said yes without hesitation. Secretly I was hoping I would like this guy enough to invite him as my date to my 35th birthday bash. I had been dreading going solo.

A day before our impending date, he texted me to say he had a surprise for me. He would not give me any clues except to remind me that he had the keys to many important buildings in the city (he was a contractor). It did not take a genius to figure out that we were going to the top of a building that had a really cool view. Leave it to a guy to not know how to keep a surprise. So typical, thinking he was so smooth when in fact he was anything but. Now which building we were going to, I was not sure. But it was definitely a building. And it was definitely going to include a cool view.

I met him for dinner in the South Loop, closer to where he lived. He said he had been working really long hours and it would be a lot easier on him if I came down there. I agreed to this as I had not spent much time down in that area of Chicago and I certainly had never been to the restaurant he chose. I was always up for a new experience especially when there was food involved.

As I opened the door to the restaurant, I actually felt nervous, a feeling I had not had in a long time prior to a first date. I couldn't quite place why I was feeling the way I was – Was it because it had been a while since I had been out with a guy I met online? Was it because I sensed there really could be something between us? Or was my excitement for the big surprise later on that was presenting in the way of nerves? Unfortunately I didn't have time to figure out the answer as he was already standing by the bar with a drink in hand when I arrived. As I headed towards him, I was happy to discover he was very good-looking, and so he got a point for not looking different from his profile picture. After the maître de escorted us to our table, we sat down and got right in to good conversation. He got another point for not only being able to banter over text, but live in person as well.

And so our dinner went. At one point I do recall spacing out, taking a moment to size him up. I was pretty sure most girls did this on date one, but I had mastered it. I would nod and smile, and pretend like I was listening to the story he seemed so excited to tell; but in truth, I was picturing kissing him, trying to size up just how attracted to him I was. Could I see him interacting with my friends, followed by my family? Usually I was able to wrap up the "daydream" in time to respond to whatever it was the guy was talking about and not appear as though I had just left the table to go to some far-away land. This time was no different. And while I was not sure how I felt about this guy based on my daydream, I at least was having a pretty good time and still found I was curious about the "big surprise" he had for me.

After dinner, we took a cab to his apartment. He insisted on driving to this secret location so we had to pick up his car. While in his garage, it got very quiet. I suddenly became very aware that I was alone with a complete stranger, about to get in to his car, where he could virtually lock me in, drive me to Idaho, and kill me in the potato fields. My heart started to race. But another voice shouted louder, telling me I was nuts and to just relax. This inner conflict continued until we got to the secret building location — right in the loop on LaSalle. We pulled in to the garage and I was happy to see him wave and say hi to the various security guards. It made me feel a bit better that people recognized him. So with that, I took a deep breath, told myself that I was not part of a Lifetime movie, and I needed to relax and enjoy the rest of this evening. We definitely were not heading to Idaho.

I followed him in to the elevator and we headed up to the top floor. When the doors opened, we walked straight in to this library that had an awesome pool table, a bar and an amazing view of the city. It was definitely pretty cool, but it was also eerily quiet. No one else was up there. No one would hear if I screamed. My fear had reappeared and I found myself conflicted between giving in to my nerves or taking a deep breath and relaxing. I could stand motionless in my own panic, or I could try to have some fun. After I mulled it over for a few seconds, telling that "Elphaba" voice of mine to shut up even though she was so loud sometimes, I opted for the latter, kicked off my shoes, grabbed the pool sticks and challenged him to a game.

All seemed to be better, until I went to take my next shot.

He announced he would "be right back" and the next thing I knew, the lights had gone dim and I heard a low voice ask, "Have you ever heard of the Devil in the White City?"

I swore time stood still and I was pretty sure my heart stopped beating all together. As I gasped for air, I managed to squeak out, "Yes. But <u>why</u> are we talking about a book about serial killers?"

My mind started to race to the following two thoughts: "Nikki knows his name and had looked him up on Facebook. Thank God for her top-notch stalking abilities" and "Marissa knew I was going to the top of a building somewhere. So if anything happens to me it won't be left as a mystery and they can give the police and my Mom information…"

One-hundredth dating lesson learned: If you go out with a complete stranger, you absolutely had to make sure at least one, if not two, of your friends knew his name and the vicinity of where you would be.

My second thought was to make a run for it. But could I make it to the elevators without him catching me? Doubtful. I did not know what else to do but stand frozen in my steps as he inched his way closer to me. I must have looked absolutely terrified because when he reached me, he looked shocked.

He gave me a hug and cautiously asked, "Did I scare you?"

I was shaking so badly he would have had to be the biggest idiot on the planet to not know he scared me. Did he not realize he was a complete stranger I had only met today? Did he not realize he brought me to the top floor of a random building where there was not another soul in sight? And did he not realize he had dimmed the lights and talked about a book whose main character was a serial killer? Yeah, I would say I was pretty damn scared.

My first reaction was to let out a giggle. That was what I did when I got nervous. However, it by no means meant I was ok or that I thought the situation was actually funny. It was just the way my body handled fear. Through my nervous laugh, I was still able to make it clear that he had scared the daylights out of me. He felt terrible and claimed that he just wanted to show me the great view and discuss the architecture from the top of the building we were on.

He justified his comment by saying both of those things were also a big part of the book.

Fine. Fair enough. Between my own creative mind and watching too many made-for-TV movies, both had likely contributed to my abysmal reaction. However, it was absolutely not right for him to have done that to me in the way that he had, especially it being the first night we had ever met.

In that moment, I also realized how stupid it was of me to have gone with him to this rooftop. While things worked out in my favor (clearly he did not kill me as I lived to tell about it), it just as easily could have been a story on the 11 p.m. news "Girl falls for Serial Killer's charm on Match.com. Ends up dead on a pool table on the top floor of a building in Chicago's Loop." I still shutter thinking about it.

So while he was not a serial killer, and repeatedly told me how terrible he felt, I could not get past it. Something did not feel right and I absolutely did not trust this guy. Maybe my initial nerves prior to the date had been my intuition; maybe it was much stronger than I had ever realized. Maybe there were times "Elpheba" needed to be shushed and there were other times there was a reason she was screaming so loudly.

Once I was safe in a cab on the way back to my apartment, I knew I would never see him again. Still shaking when I arrived home, I slept with the lights on that night.

I could not believe that two days before my 35th birthday, dating had now meant I had to possibly fear for my life. Was there ever going to be an end to all of this? Had I not finally paid enough "bad dating" dues?

Interlude

"Miss Open Heart"

My sister once told me that when you ask the Universe for something, and you ask for it completely authentically with nothing but love and gratitude, it will respond and bring you what you want and need.

I literally thought she was a nut job when she told me this, and yet I found myself asking for Mr. Right — with every candle I blew out that birthday, with every prayer I prayed at night, with every quiet chance I got to ask my loved ones "up there" — I said "I'm really ready. Please bring him in to my life. Whoever he is, I welcome him with open arms." And in that moment, I felt a sense of relief. I had grown so exhausted by all the years of effort I had put in that I decided it was time to let go and turn it over to a much higher power.

A weight had been lifted, and I suddenly experienced a sense of freedom like never before.

On the Friday of Labor Day Weekend 2012, my company was closing early for the holiday so I decided to make lunch plans with Mr. Chicago. Oh yeah, I probably should mention that somewhere between Mr. Cobweb Cleaner and Mr. Alcharexic, he and I had gotten back in touch and had become friends. My LinkedIn profile had continued to show up on his as "someone you may know". At some point he clicked on it and discovered I was now living in Chicago, which prompted him to send me an email to see how I was. From that point on we would get together for lunch every couple of months. We had become, for lack of a better title, "lunch buddies".

Anyway, he and I had not seen each other in a few months, and were overdue to catch up. We decided to go to Cantina Laredo for some good Mexican food and inevitably some potent margaritas. Over the years, I had gone from being able to keep up with the boys to becoming a lightweight. Needless to say, about one-and-a-half drinks in and I was drunk — yet we stayed in our booth for about five hours. We caught up on life, I told him about my last date with Mr. Devil in the White City and he shook his head at my stupidity. We chatted about the surgery he had just had and the second one coming up, we talked about our friends and families — we just talked away. The ease between us when it came to conversation never went away, so we could go a few months without seeing each other and pick right back up where we left off each time. There was something comforting about having that with someone. And after all I had recently been through from fearing my own life on a first date, to not quite feeling like myself or connected to men (other than the few hot few hours I had spent with Mr. Music), *it felt really good.*

By hour six, it was time for me to head out to meet some friends. I was having a ton of fun and did not want to leave, but I had told them I would be there and I was a woman of my word. So we said our goodbyes, I got in a cab, and suddenly I felt like myself again. I knew I could go out that night with my friends and be the best version of myself. It felt so good to be back and I had Mr. Chicago *to thank. Go figure.*

Shortly after our lunch, I helped Mr. Chicago *find a new job. He had revealed how badly he needed a change and I really felt he would do phenomenally well in my industry selling digital media. Because I was helping him with this endeavor, we started to speak much more regularly. We were in contact almost daily, which was a pretty drastic shift from what it had been the last two years. And while you would think this would, and should, scare and concern me, it would be so easy for us to fall back in to the past with potential to relive a situation that ended so poorly, it did not. I was comfortable and happy.*

Of course it did beg the question — can you really be very close friends with an ex that you were truly in love with? Despite the fact most people would argue the answer was absolutely not, mine was absolutely yes.

So as Mr. Chicago *and I talked more and more, it <u>was</u> a shock to me when I came to the conclusion I still loved him. During one of our lunches earlier that same year I had* *adamantly proclaimed: "I would never get back together with you. That ship has sailed and too much has happened". At the time he shook his head and with a sheepish smile said, "Sure Court." But I ignored it, because I truly meant what I said — that day.*

One hundred and first dating lesson learned: Regardless of the mind, the heart wants what the heart wants.

As we entered the month of November, and my feelings were now very present, I realized I was going to have to come out and tell him how I was feeling. I had to get it off my chest, with no expectations other than to be honest with him and more importantly, with myself. If I was going to have my heart open and truly ready for Mr. Right to walk in, then I had to be honest about any feelings I was having. I had finally realized being in touch with my emotions and being real with myself was the only way the Universe was going to bring me what I kept asking for.

On November 7, 2012, Mr. Chicago took me to dinner to thank me for helping him get a new job. We went to a terrific trendy sushi restaurant in Chicago's Wicker Park neighborhood where we shared a number of amazing dishes, some delicious wine and, as always, great conversation.

As the night came to an end, and he was about to put me in a cab, he stopped and said, "What's up Court? You have something to say? I know you all too well."

JESUS CHRIST! I could not get away with anything when it came to this guy. Was I that obvious? Did I have that poor a poker face? Or did he really and truly just know me as well as he believed? No matter the answer, there was no turning back now: it was definitely now or never.

We headed to his car to talk, I settled in to the passenger's seat, took a deep breath, and then blurted it all out in one constant torrent:

"I still love you and you don't have to say anything but I just wanted to tell you and I'm not saying let's get back together because that would be too much pressure right now, but..."

Before I could continue with my 200-word run-on statement, he kissed me. And it all came rushing back — the chemistry, the passion, the intensity and, inevitably, the love.

Now before you get ahead of yourselves, this was not where this book ends. My dating life, and the triple digit dating lessons it taught me was way too complex for it to wrap up that neatly. After all, I did not say I wanted to get back together with Mr. Chicago. I just simply needed to tell him I still loved him so that I could be true and authentic with my feelings in general. How my life and love story was going to turn out was still unknown.

And while a huge weight had been lifted off of my chest — realizing I could admit my feelings, feel good about them, not be afraid to share them, and for them to be well received — the reality was we had been down this road a few times now. I knew I needed to proceed with a lot of *caution because as the saying goes, "Fool me once, shame on you. Fool me twice, shame on me".*

This aforementioned quote was one that I took to heart. I had no interest in being shamed and certainly not after everything I had been through in the last 10 years. I was no fool.

Instead, I was going to remain open. I was going to allow this part of my life to play itself out. If something was supposed to happen with Mr. Chicago, then it would. And if not, well then there was going to be someone else. But no matter what, I was finally relinquishing control and letting the universe take over. It was time. And it felt really good.

The Prince

"Mr. Right"

The next few months were interesting in that *Mr. Chicago* and I continued to grow closer — both emotionally and professionally — now that he was in my industry and we had to work together. But we were very careful physically. Kissing was as far as we would go until we knew if we were going to commit to being together.

We both wanted and needed to be sure. And while the feelings, chemistry, connection and love were all there; we also had the knowledge — and the pain — of what it was like to break up. We also knew we were not going to turn back in to "lunch buddies" after this go around. Failure this time would mean having to cut all ties forever.

So before we crossed the line, we both needed to feel 100 percent sure. And that certainly was not typical for the way relationships would often build. Most of my friends that had ended up in relationships more recently had jumped in head first with no looking back. We did not have that luxury, but then again, because of our history, we had that luxury. We were patient, authentic, and truly honest with each other for the next few months that followed.

Back in the year 2000, I was in the Hallmark store looking for some birthday cards for my Mom when I stumbled upon one in the "love" section that struck me in a way that I knew I had no choice but to buy it. The words written described exactly what I wanted in a relationship and a true partner in life. At the time, I bought it with *Mr. Almost But Not Quite Right* in mind, as that was who I was in a relationship with; however, something held me back from ever giving it to him, and as we all now know, that relationship ended a year later. Instead I held on to this very special card with the hopes that I would one day be able to give it to the man I would eventually spend my life with. The card moved with me from my apartment in Union City, to both New York City apartments I lived in, and eventually crossed states lines to Chicago, all the while staying tucked away in my nightstand.

Mr. Chicago and I had just pulled up to Alinea, one of the top restaurants in the world, where we decided to pay an absurd amount of money to enjoy their 10+ courses tasting menu. I stopped him from getting out of the car, pulled out my Hallmark card from the year 2000, explained the history behind it, and then … yes folks, I handed it to him. It was on March 7, 2013, thirteen years after I had purchased it, and four months to the day from when I had revealed I still loved him.

To say he was touched was an understatement; and it was that moment that completely validated it was the decision to have waited to give this card to the right person, at the right time (please note, as much as I loved him the first time we dated, I had not given it to him even then).

Yes folks, we were officially back together! And furthermore, *Mr. Chicago* officially became my long awaited *Mr. Right*.

One hundred and second dating lesson learned: Timing may not be everything, but it damn sure was a lot.

The truth was, had we stayed together four years earlier, we would never had made it and actually "found" each other. We were not the same people we were when we were trying to figure out a long-distance relationship some 1,400 days earlier. We would not have learned the lessons we did in the time we spent apart. We would not be the people we were on that fateful day in March. Simply put, we would not have been able to come back together as better versions of ourselves. And it was those versions that had found each other this time. This was something we both believed to be 100 percent true. And because we were both finally in the right place to be open to receiving the love we both wanted and deserved, much to our pleasant surprise, we were able to naturally find and come back to each other.

My *Mr. Right* was, for all intents and purposes, recycled. He was not one, but multiple chapters in this book. And in reading those chapters, and as I continued having the experiences I had after our tough break up, never in a million years would I have thought he would be who I was writing about in this final chapter.

In the end, I was lucky enough to find the love of my life and the perfect person for me (and vice versa for him). While it was not an easy journey, I can say good things do come to those who wait and there is definitely a lot of truth in the well-known saying "patience is a virtue".

I truly believed it was my journey of dating stories that allowed me to finally get to where I am today, even if I couldn't say that while I was actually living them. And for all of that, for every last piece of it, I feel blessed.

My relationship is fulfilling in so many ways — I am with the person who can make me laugh so hard my stomach hurts, the person who I can talk to about anything and everything, the person who I can stand in front of and know he knows and sees me for exactly who I am (and I him). It is wonderful to know we choose to be with each other each and every day because we want to be — despite all of our flaws — and that we love each other deeply, imperfections and all. I am with the person who I can talk rationally about our issues, have an immense physical and emotional connection to, the person whose mere hug can make the world feel like it does not exist. I am with my best friend. And I only wish each and every one of you find the strength and courage to hold out for that person too. Because if you do, I can promise you, the reward far exceeds anything else.

On January 5, 2014, Mike (yes that is *Mr. Chicago turned Mr. Right's* real name) proposed to me when we were on vacation in St. Martin. And true to the statement that the "best laid plans often go awry," he had a few different elaborate ways he wanted to pop the question that included things like a private beach or a bathtub full of rose pedals.

None of those things happened due to various circumstances so when it came down to it, he proposed when it was just "us" in the middle of a moment, standing alone in our hotel room in our bathing suits, with me soaking wet from the rain storm I had just gotten caught in moments before. I could not think of a better way to have someone I love so much ask to make us "forever."

Eight months later, on August 31, 2014, we were married in Chicago surrounded by our closest family and friends. It was a beautiful and amazing day filled with smiles, laughter, and a lot of dancing. Marissa's life-long dream to be my Matron of Honor, along with her two daughters as my flower girls, had come true and to this day I am not sure who was beaming more, her or my Mom.

I believe the moral of our story was simply that it was <u>ours</u>. This was what was supposed to happen for us. This was our path, Mike and mine. We had done the work on ourselves as individuals, we happened to each land on what we wanted out of a "forever relationship," and naturally came back together.

I have been blessed and lucky enough to find my happy beginning. And yes I said beginning and not ending. I chose those words specifically, as my belief has never been "and she lived happily ever after." I learned early on that meeting the man of my dreams did not mean the rest of my life would then be wrapped up in a pretty box with a bow on top. If that is what you are looking for, throw in the towel now, because that is not reality. Reality was and is finding the person who was perfect for me to partner with to go through, side by side, all of the ups AND downs life often throws at us. And while he, nor I, nor our relationship, nor the path we had to both take to get here was or is perfect, we are perfect for each other and that is what makes what we have perfection. I like to call it imperfectly perfect.

Conclusion

"Bless The Broken Road"

When I started this book, I honestly did not know if I would ever find the one. There were many days throughout the years when I figured I might just be someone who may not ever get married. Someone who my family members may have decided was way too picky; or worse, thought I was a lesbian and believed the girls I was taking vacations with were actually my lovers. Yes, I was <u>that</u> girl.

So for those of you out there who are feeling the same way, please know you are not alone. While I cannot claim to be the predictor of your future, never give up on yourself or love if that is what you truly want for yourself. There is no reason to be afraid to be honest or own that this is a desire you seek. And while it may take longer than you initially decided it should, when it is your turn, it will have been worth the wait; that I can promise you.

For those of you out there who are feeling like dating has become like a job, that you will never find your "perfection" and are destined to be single forever — the reality of that may all be true. I cannot and will not be one of those people who pretend now that I found my love, all of a sudden I have the right to tell you with 100-percent certainty that you will too. The truth is that the only certain thing in life IS uncertainty.

But I do hope you take the message that finding your true love <u>is</u> possible and because of <u>that</u>, you should never ever give up on love. I hope that my story can bring hope; that sticking it out for the right person is well worth the wait. If you do the work on yourself and know yourself, stay true to yourself and hold out for what you know works for you, you have a much better chance of finding happiness in a relationship.

What I CAN say with 100 percent certainty is that if you are lucky enough to find it, you will be able to look back and be thankful you waited, be thankful for all of the hardships and ups and downs, be thankful for all that you experienced, and even be thankful for all of those frogs you had to kiss first. For without all of that, it would not be possible for you to be the best version of you and the best person you can be in the relationship you want to be in.

I still have not figured out why exactly it takes some people a lot of work and effort in this department and why others seem to find love so much more easily. If I knew the answer to that question, I would have been retired three times over by now and penning this novel from a beach. But I realized it doesn't really matter. The truth is, we are all on our own journey. And I believe every single one of us is exactly where we are meant to be. If you can take on that outlook and belief system, you may be able to focus a bit more on enjoying the ride versus arriving at the destination.

Try to compartmentalize as best you can when it comes to your feelings; you can have your "I'm not sure I'll ever find it" box as long as you don't ever throw away your "letting loose and enjoying your freedom to travel, go out and enjoy life" box. The two can live mutually exclusive within you. I found it so liberating and helpful when I was finally able to come to that realization.

The only trepidation I have in sharing my personal story has been that the wrong message would be received: And that is that there's hope for you and an ex. The message and point of this book <u>was not</u> and <u>should not</u> be that. I sincerely do not encourage people to go back or hold out hope. The truth is, if a break up occurred, it likely happened for good reason. And if you end up having a similar story to mine, it will not be because you sat around and waited and hoped, but because you explored and grew. You changed and transformed, and found what it was that you needed and what you could give.

With that, I leave you with these five key things to strongly consider and try your best to live by:

1) Keep your heart open;
2) Focus on remaining true and authentic;
3) Relinquish control;
4) Try hard not to dwell too much, and definitely do not beat yourself up over what you could have done better or differently in a failed relationship; take what you learned and apply it to your next one.
5) Your story will unfold exactly as it is supposed to. Have faith and trust in THAT.

And last but certainly not least, the final dedication that I promised in the very beginning but didn't want to give away:

To Mike, for loving me and for choosing to do so each and every day, for never letting a day by without telling me how much you love me, for letting me be me, for being my best friend, and of course, for being patient over these last few months as I obsessed and made edit after edit after edit to this book!

With all my love, and a few kisses from frogs,
Courtney

www.ingramcontent.com/pod-product-compliance
Lightning Source LLC
LaVergne TN
LVHW041316080426
835513LV00008B/479